CHINESE IR
STRATEGY FOR
MULTILATERALISM
A BOOK BY
CALEB MAINA IDI
2023

CHINESE IR STRATEGY FOR MULTILATERALISM

Table of Contents

1.0 **Introduction**

1.0.1 **Understanding Chinese Foreign Policy**

1.1 The Rise of China

1.2 The Concept of Multilateralism

1.3 Chinese Foreign Policy Priorities

Part I: Historical Context

2. Historical Evolution of Chinese IR Strategy

2.1 Traditional Chinese Foreign Policy Principles

2.2 Maoist Era and Isolationism

2.3 Deng Xiaoping and the Opening Up

2.4 Post-Deng Xiaoping Era and Global Engagement

Part II: Foundations of Chinese Multilateralism

3. China's Participation in International Organizations

3.1 China's Role in the United Nations

3.2 China and Regional Organizations (ASEAN, SCO)

3.3 China's Membership in Economic Institutions (WTO, AIIB)

China's Approach to Multilateral Diplomacy

4.1 Principles Guiding China's Multilateral Engagement

4.2 Multilateralism with Chinese Characteristics

4.3 The Belt and Road Initiative (BRI) and Multilateral Cooperation

Part III: Key Areas of Chinese Multilateral Engagement

5. Economic Multilateralism

5.1 China's Trade and Investment Policies

5.2 China's Role in Global Economic Governance

5.3 Chinese-Led Economic Initiatives (RCEP, CPTPP)

Security Multilateralism

6.1 China's Defense and Security Policies

6.2 China's Participation in Arms Control and Non-Proliferation

6.3 Regional Security Cooperation in Asia-Pacific

Climate Change and Environmental Multilateralism

7.1 China's Environmental Challenges

7.2 China's Climate Change Policies

7.3 China's Role in International Climate Negotiations

Part IV: Challenges and Opportunities

8. Balancing National Interests and Global Responsibilities

8.1 Sovereignty Concerns and National Interests

8.2 Chinese Leadership in Multilateral Institutions

8.3 Managing Geopolitical Tensions in Multilateralism

Perception and Trust Building

9.1 Chinese Soft Power and Public Diplomacy

9.2 Challenges in Perception Management

9.3 Building Trust and Enhancing Cooperation

Conclusion

10. Assessing China's Multilateralism

10.1 Achievements and Criticisms

10.2 Future Prospects and Challenges

Glossary

References

Introduction

In today's interconnected and interdependent global landscape, multilateralism has emerged as a vital principle for addressing complex challenges and promoting cooperation among nations. As one of the major global powers, China has been actively shaping its foreign policy and international relations (IR) strategy with a strong emphasis on multilateralism. This essay aims to provide a comprehensive analysis of China's IR strategy for multilateralism, examining its objectives, motivations, key initiatives, and challenges. By delving into this topic, we can gain a deeper understanding of China's role in the evolving international order and its approach to global governance.

Understanding Multilateralism:

To set the foundation for our analysis, it is crucial to grasp the concept of multilateralism. Multilateralism refers to a system or approach where multiple states work together to address common challenges and pursue shared goals through international organizations, treaties, and agreements. It is characterized by the principles of inclusiveness, consensus-building, and the recognition of the sovereign equality of states. Multilateralism provides a framework for collective decision-making, cooperation, and the pursuit of common interests in various areas such as trade, security, environment, and global development.

China's Emergence as a Global Power:
Over the past few decades, China has witnessed remarkable economic growth and development, propelling it to the forefront of global affairs. As a rising power, China's foreign policy has undergone significant transformations, evolving from a largely inward-looking approach to a more proactive and assertive stance on the global stage. In recent years,

China has recognized the importance of multilateralism as a means to secure its interests, enhance its international standing, and shape the global order to align with its vision.

Objectives of China's Multilateralism Strategy:
China's IR strategy for multilateralism is guided by a set of specific objectives. Firstly, China seeks to safeguard its national interests, including territorial integrity, economic prosperity, and social stability, by actively engaging with the international community. Secondly, China aims to promote a more inclusive, balanced, and multipolar global order that accommodates the aspirations and interests of emerging powers. Thirdly, China endeavors to establish itself as a responsible global leader by contributing to global governance, addressing global challenges, and playing a constructive role in international institutions.

Motivations behind China's Multilateralism Strategy:

Several motivations underpin China's pursuit of multilateralism. One crucial factor is the recognition of the limitations of unilateralism and the need for collective action in addressing complex global issues such as climate change, global health pandemics, terrorism, and nuclear proliferation. By engaging in multilateral mechanisms, China can share the burdens and responsibilities of global governance while mitigating the risks of hegemonic dominance by any single power. Additionally, China's multilateral approach is also driven by its desire to shape international norms, rules, and institutions to reflect its interests and values, fostering a more equitable and balanced world order.

Key Initiatives in China's Multilateralism Strategy:
China has implemented various initiatives to strengthen its multilateral engagement and influence. One prominent example is the Belt and Road Initiative (BRI), a massive infrastructure and connectivity project that aims to enhance regional

and global economic integration. Through BRI, China seeks to establish partnerships with participating countries, improve connectivity, promote trade, and enhance people-to-people exchanges. This initiative showcases China's commitment to economic multilateralism and its willingness to collaborate with other nations to achieve shared prosperity.

China's engagement with regional and international organizations is another crucial aspect of its multilateralism strategy. China actively participates in organizations such as the United Nations (UN), World Trade Organization (WTO), Shanghai Cooperation Organization (SCO), and BRICS (Brazil,Russia, India, China, and South Africa) to shape decision-making processes, advocate for its interests, and strengthen its influence within these institutions. China also plays an active role in regional multilateral frameworks, including the Association of Southeast Asian Nations (ASEAN) and the Asia-Pacific Economic Cooperation (APEC), to foster regional cooperation and integration.

Moreover, China has been a vocal supporter of free trade and economic globalization. In the face of rising protectionism and trade disputes, China has championed multilateral trade mechanisms, such as the WTO, and has called for the reform and improvement of global trade rules to ensure fairness, inclusiveness, and mutual benefits for all parties involved. China's commitment to economic multilateralism is further demonstrated by its active involvement in initiatives like the Regional Comprehensive Economic Partnership (RCEP), a mega-trade deal involving 15 countries in the Asia-Pacific region.

Furthermore, China has increasingly engaged in multilateral dialogues and diplomacy to promote peace and stability in international relations. It has played a pivotal role in the negotiations surrounding the Iranian nuclear deal (Joint

Comprehensive Plan of Action) and has been actively involved in the Six-Party Talks on the denuclearization of the Korean Peninsula. China's mediation efforts and diplomatic engagement aim to address regional security challenges and foster a cooperative and inclusive approach to conflict resolution.

Challenges and Criticisms:
China's pursuit of multilateralism is not without challenges and criticisms. One major challenge lies in reconciling its aspirations for a more multipolar global order with existing power structures and the interests of established powers, particularly the United States. The competition for influence and the potential clash of interests between China and other major powers can impede the smooth functioning of multilateral mechanisms and hinder effective global governance.

Moreover, China's growing influence has raised concerns among some countries about its intentions and the potential for a power imbalance. Critics argue that China's multilateral initiatives, such as the BRI, may be driven by strategic interests and could lead to economic dependency or debt vulnerabilities for participating countries. There are also concerns about China's adherence to international norms, human rights, and its approach to issues like territorial disputes in the South China Sea.

China's domestic policies and governance practices have also faced scrutiny, particularly in relation to issues such as human rights, freedom of expression, and intellectual property rights. These concerns can impact China's credibility and influence within multilateral institutions and affect its ability to effectively advocate for its interests.

Implications for the Global Order:
China's multilateralism strategy has significant implications for the evolving global order. Its growing engagement and influence within

international organizations and regional frameworks have the potential to reshape global governance and decision-making processes. As China seeks a greater voice in global affairs, the dynamics of power and influence within multilateral institutions may shift, requiring adjustments in the traditional balance of power.

China's emphasis on economic multilateralism, through initiatives like the BRI and RCEP, also signals a shift in the global economic landscape. By promoting connectivity, trade liberalization, and economic integration, China aims to expand its markets, enhance its economic influence, and shape regional and global economic rules to better reflect its interests. This could lead to alternative models of economic cooperation and competition, potentially challenging the dominance of Western-led economic institutions.

Furthermore, China's multilateralism strategy can have implications for the norms and values that underpin the international system. As China becomes more influential in shaping global governance, there may be debates and contestation over issues such as human rights, democracy, and the rule of law. Balancing diverse perspectives and interests within multilateral institutions will be crucial to ensuring inclusive and effective global governance.

China's IR strategy for multilateralism is an integral component of its foreign policy and global engagement. By actively participating in international organizations,treaties, and initiatives, China aims to secure its national interests, promote a multipolar world order, and contribute to global governance. Its key initiatives, such as the Belt and Road Initiative and participation in regional and international organizations, highlight its commitment to economic multilateralism, regional cooperation, and conflict resolution. However, China's multilateralism strategy also faces challenges and criticisms, including concerns about power imbalances, adherence to international norms, and governance practices.

The implications of China's multilateralism strategy are far-reaching, affecting the global order, economic landscape, and norms in international relations. As China's influence within multilateral institutions grows, the dynamics of power and decision-making may shift, necessitating adaptations in the existing global governance structures. China's emphasis on economic multilateralism could potentially challenge the dominance of Western-led institutions, leading to alternative models of economic cooperation and competition. Moreover, debates and contestation over issues such as human rights, democracy, and the rule of law are likely to arise as China becomes more influential in shaping global governance.

Understanding China's IR strategy for multilateralism is crucial for comprehending its role in the evolving international order and the dynamics of global governance. By examining its objectives, motivations, key initiatives, and challenges, we gain valuable insights into China's approach to multilateralism and its implications for the global system. It is essential for policymakers, scholars, and practitioners to engage in nuanced analysis and dialogue to foster a more inclusive and cooperative international environment that accommodates diverse interests and values while addressing the complex challenges of the 21st century.

Understanding Chinese Foreign Policy

In recent decades, China's rise as a global power has been accompanied by significant changes in its foreign policy. As the world's second-largest economy and a permanent member of the United Nations Security Council, China's foreign policy decisions have far-reaching implications for global politics, trade, and security. Understanding the underlying motivations, principles, and strategies that guide Chinese foreign policy is crucial for comprehending its impact on regional and global dynamics.

This comprehensive introduction aims to provide a thorough analysis of Chinese foreign policy, exploring its historical context, core principles, key actors, and evolving strategies. By examining China's diplomatic approach, regional ambitions, economic initiatives, and security concerns, we can gain valuable insights into the country's current and future international behavior.

Historical Context

To understand China's foreign policy, one must recognize the historical factors that have shaped its worldview and approach to international relations. China's long history as a centralized empire, coupled with periods of relative isolation, has influenced its perception of its role in the world.

The country's experiences with imperialism and the humiliation of the Opium Wars have left a lasting impact on its national psyche.

In the mid-20th century, China underwent significant political and ideological transformations, marked by the founding of the People's Republic of China in 1949 under Communist Party rule. Mao Zedong's leadership during this era was characterized by an emphasis on self-reliance and the promotion of revolutionary movements worldwide. However, Deng Xiaoping's economic reforms in the late 1970s initiated a new phase in Chinese foreign policy, focusing on economic development and international integration.

Core Principles

Chinese foreign policy is guided by a set of core principles that reflect its historical experiences, cultural values, and national interests. These principles provide a framework for understanding China's approach to international relations and its interactions with other countries. The following principles are central to Chinese foreign policy:

Sovereignty: China places great importance on territorial integrity and national sovereignty. It asserts its right to make independent decisions and resist external interference in its internal affairs, particularly on sensitive issues like Tibet, Taiwan, and Hong Kong.

Non-Interference: China adheres to the principle of non-interference in the domestic affairs of other countries, a stance rooted in its own experience with Western intervention. This principle is often used to deflect criticism of China's human rights record or its relations with authoritarian regimes.

Peaceful Development: China advocates for peaceful coexistence and emphasizes economic development as a means to achieve stability and prosperity. The concept of "win-win" cooperation is frequently promoted in its economic partnerships and international initiatives, such as the Belt and Road Initiative.

Harmonious World: China aspires to create a harmonious world order characterized by mutual respect, cooperation, and the pursuit of common development. It seeks to enhance its global influence through diplomatic engagement, multilateralism, and the promotion of a multipolar international system.

Key Actors

To comprehend Chinese foreign policy, it is essential to identify the key actors and institutions involved in its formulation and implementation. The Chinese Communist Party (CCP) holds ultimate authority over foreign policy decisions, with the paramount leader exerting significant influence. The Ministry of Foreign Affairs (MFA) is responsible for conducting diplomatic relations and negotiating agreements, while the People's Liberation Army (PLA) plays a vital role in safeguarding China's security interests.

Additionally, China's increasing involvement in global governance has led to the establishment of various specialized institutions and platforms. These include the National Development and Reform Commission (NDRC), responsible for economic planning, and the Shanghai Cooperation Organization (SCO), which fosters regional cooperation among Eurasian countries.

Evolving Strategies

China's foreign policy strategies have evolved over time to align with its changing economic, political, and security priorities. Under Deng Xiaoping's leadership in the 1980s, China began to prioritize economic development and integration into the global economy. This led to a focus on export-led growth, foreign investment, and the establishment of economic partnerships and trade agreements.

In the 2000s, China's economic growth and expanding global influence spurred a more assertive foreign policy posture. This was characterized by a greater emphasis on securing resources, protecting its overseas citizens and assets, and defending its territorial claims. The Chinese government also began to pursue a more active role in regional and global governance, establishing new platforms such as the Asian Infrastructure Investment Bank (AIIB) and the New Development Bank (NDB).

In recent years, China's foreign policy has become increasingly confrontational with the United States and its allies, reflecting a growing sense of rivalry and competition. The Belt and Road Initiative, launched in 2013, is a flagship economic project aimed at increasing China's influence in the Asia-Pacific region and beyond. However, concerns about the project's debt sustainability, environmental impact, and strategic implications have led to skepticism and criticism from some countries.

China's territorial claims in the South China Sea and its militarization of disputed islands have also raised tensions in the region and strained its relations with neighboring countries. China's human rights record, particularly its treatment of ethnic minorities in Xinjiang and its crackdown on dissent in Hong Kong, has also drawn international condemnation.

In conclusion, understanding Chinese foreign policy is critical to comprehending its global impact and predicting its future behavior. China's historical experiences, cultural values, and national interests have shaped its core principles and approach to international relations. The key actors involved in formulating and implementing foreign policy include the CCP, the MFA, and the PLA, while specialized institutions and platforms have been established to promote economic, political, and security goals.

China's foreign policy strategies have evolved over time, reflecting its changing economic, political, and security priorities. While economic development and integration into the global economy have been a central focus, China's growing global influence has led to a more assertive posture, characterized by a greater emphasis on securing resources, protecting its overseas citizens and assets, and defending its territorial claims.

The rise of China as a global power has also led to increasing competition and rivalry with the United States and its allies. As China's influence continues to grow, it is likely that its foreign policy will become even more assertive and confrontational in the years ahead. Understanding these dynamics is essential for policymakers, scholars, and businesses seeking to navigate the complex landscape of global politics and economics.

The Rise of China: A Global Power Emerges

The 21st century has witnessed a remarkable transformation in the global geopolitical landscape, with China's emergence as a dominant player on the world stage. The rise of China has become one of the most significant and consequential developments of our time, reshaping the global balance of power and challenging existing international norms. This essay aims to provide an in-depth analysis of the factors contributing to China's rise, the implications it has for the international system, and the challenges it poses to established powers and the existing global order.

Historical Perspective: China's Resilience and Rejuvenation

To understand the rise of China, it is essential to examine its historical context. China has a rich and ancient civilization that has endured for millennia, witnessing periods of great prosperity as well as tumultuous times. However, the country experienced a century of humiliation at the hands of foreign powers during the 19th and early 20th centuries, which profoundly shaped its national consciousness. The Chinese Communist Party's rise to power in 1949 marked the beginning of a new era, characterized by efforts to rejuvenate the nation and regain its past glory.

Economic Transformation: From Deng Xiaoping to Xi Jinping

China's remarkable economic growth and transformation since the late 1970s have been central to its rise as a global power. Under the leadership of Deng Xiaoping, China embraced market-oriented economic reforms, opening up to foreign investment and trade. This shift resulted in rapid industrialization, urbanization, and the lifting of millions out of poverty. Deng's policies laid the foundation for China's integration into the global economy.

The subsequent leadership, including Jiang Zemin, Hu Jintao, and currently Xi Jinping, continued to prioritize economic development as a key objective. China's sustained high levels of economic growth, fueled by a combination of state-led industrialization, export-oriented manufacturing, and massive domestic consumption, propelled the nation to become the world's second-largest economy. China's Belt and Road Initiative (BRI) and the establishment of the Asian Infrastructure Investment Bank (AIIB) further underscore its ambition to expand its economic influence globally.

Technological Advancement: The Fourth Industrial Revolution

China's rise is not limited to its economic prowess but also encompasses its rapid technological advancements. The country has made substantial investments in research and development, leading to breakthroughs in areas such as artificial intelligence (AI), quantum computing, 5G technology, and space exploration. China's focus on technological innovation is evident through initiatives like "Made in China 2025," which aims to upgrade the country's manufacturing capabilities and foster indigenous innovation.

Moreover, China's leading technology companies, such as Alibaba, Tencent, and Huawei, have gained global prominence, challenging traditional Western technological dominance. The rise of China's tech giants has raised concerns regarding data privacy, cybersecurity, and intellectual property rights, leading to debates about the implications of China's technological rise for global governance and security.

Military Modernization: Shifting Power Dynamics

China's rise as a global power is accompanied by its military modernization efforts. The People's Liberation Army (PLA) has undergone significant reforms, prioritizing the development of advanced capabilities in areas such as cyber warfare, space technology, naval expansion, and ballistic missile systems. China's military modernization has not only enhanced its ability to protect its territorial integrity but has also expanded its influence in regional security affairs, challenging the dominance of the United States and its allies in the Asia-Pacific region.

China's assertiveness in territorial disputes in the South China Sea and its increasing military presence in the Indian Ocean have raised concerns among neighboring countries and global powers alike. The military balance in the Asia-Pacific region is shifting, leading to complex strategic calculations and the potential for heightened tensions

Geopolitical Ambitions: A New Global Order?

China's rise is accompanied by a growing desire to assert itself on the global stage and reshape the existing international order. The Belt and Road Initiative (BRI), often referred to as China's modern-day Silk Road, is a prime example of its geopolitical ambitions. This massive infrastructure development project aims to connect Asia, Europe, and Africa through a network of transportation, energy, and telecommunications routes. By investing in infrastructure projects across continents, China seeks to enhance its economic influence, create new markets, and establish stronger political ties with participating countries.

Furthermore, China's increasing engagement in multilateral institutions and initiatives, such as the AIIB, Shanghai Cooperation Organization (SCO), and the Regional Comprehensive Economic Partnership (RCEP), demonstrates its efforts to shape global governance mechanisms to align with its interests. These developments raise questions about the future trajectory of international institutions and the potential for a shift in global power dynamics.

While China's rise presents opportunities, it also poses challenges and risks for both its domestic stability and the international community. Domestically, China faces issues such as income inequality, environmental degradation, an aging population, and the need to balance economic growth with social stability. The Chinese government's control over information flow and restrictions on civil liberties have drawn criticism, leading to concerns about human rights and political freedom.

On the international front, China's assertive behavior in territorial disputes, its controversial approach to intellectual property rights, and its expanding military capabilities have created tensions with neighboring countries and raised concerns among established powers. As China's influence grows, questions about its intentions and whether it will adhere to established international norms and rules become crucial.

Implications for Established Powers and Global Order

China's rise challenges the dominance of established powers, particularly the United States, in various arenas. Economically, China's emergence as a manufacturing hub and its increasing technological capabilities have disrupted global supply chains and reshaped industries worldwide. The trade tensions between China and the United States, epitomized by the ongoing trade war, highlight the underlying competition for economic supremacy.

Furthermore, China's growing diplomatic influence, particularly in developing countries, challenges the traditional spheres of influence of Western powers. The competition for resources, markets, and geopolitical influence between China and other major powers like the United States and Russia is reshaping the dynamics of international relations.

Cooperation and Engagement: Finding Common Ground

In the face of China's rise, finding avenues for cooperation and engagement becomes imperative. The challenges posed by issues like climate change, global health crises, and terrorism necessitate collaborative efforts among major powers. Engaging with China on these global challenges requires a delicate balance between competition and cooperation.

Multilateral institutions, such as the United Nations, World Trade Organization, and regional organizations, can provide platforms for dialogue and negotiation. Encouraging China's adherence to international norms and rules while addressing its concerns and interests can help establish a stable and predictable global order.

China's rise as a global power represents a significant shift in the geopolitical landscape of the 21st century. Its economic transformation, technological advancements, military modernization, and geopolitical ambitions have positioned it as a major player on the world stage. The implications of China's rise for established powers and the global order are far-reaching, requiring careful navigation and strategic engagement.

The rise of China presents both opportunities and challenges. It is essential for the international community to understand the complexities of China's rise, engage in constructive dialogue, and work towards a cooperative framework that promotes peace, stability, and shared prosperity. As China continues to shape the future, the dynamics of global politics and the balance of power will undoubtedly be transformed, impacting nations and individuals around the world.

The Concept of Multilateralism: Fostering Global Cooperation for a Sustainable Future

In an interconnected world facing complex challenges, the concept of multilateralism has emerged as a vital framework for global cooperation and problem-solving. Multilateralism represents a collaborative approach that involves multiple nations coming together to address common issues, negotiate agreements, and pursue shared objectives. It recognizes that global problems, such as climate change, economic inequality, terrorism, and pandemics, transcend national borders and require collective action.

This introductory essay explores the concept of multilateralism, its historical development, principles, and key institutions. It delves into the benefits, challenges, and criticisms associated with multilateral approaches, and highlights its relevance in today's ever-changing world. Furthermore, this essay underscores the importance of multilateralism in addressing pressing global issues and fostering a sustainable future for all.

I. Historical Development of Multilateralism

Multilateralism has its roots in the aftermath of World War II, where the devastation caused by the war underscored the need for international collaboration to prevent future conflicts. The creation of the United Nations (UN) in 1945 marked a significant milestone in the promotion of multilateralism as a means to maintain global peace and security. The UN's founding charter aimed to establish a platform for member states to engage in diplomacy, negotiate solutions to disputes, and promote respect for human rights.

The subsequent years witnessed the development of various multilateral institutions, such as the World Trade Organization (WTO), International Monetary Fund (IMF), and World Bank, which aimed to facilitate economic cooperation, promote development, and address global trade imbalances. These institutions played a crucial role in fostering multilateral approaches to global challenges and creating a framework for international governance.

II. Principles of Multilateralism

Multilateralism operates based on a set of fundamental principles that guide its functioning and decision-making processes. These principles include:

Sovereign Equality: Multilateralism recognizes the sovereign equality of all member states, regardless of their size, wealth, or power. It provides an inclusive platform where all nations have an equal voice in shaping global policies and addressing shared challenges.

Collective Decision-Making: Multilateralism promotes collective decision-making, wherein member states engage in dialogue, negotiation, and consensus-building to reach agreements. This process encourages the pooling of diverse perspectives, expertise, and resources to develop solutions that are more comprehensive and representative.

Rule of Law: Multilateralism emphasizes the importance of the rule of law in international relations. Treaties, agreements, and resolutions provide a legal framework that guides member states' behavior, ensuring predictability, stability, and accountability in their interactions.

Peaceful Conflict Resolution: Multilateralism advocates for the peaceful resolution of conflicts through diplomacy, negotiation, and dialogue. It offers a platform for dialogue and mediation to prevent and resolve disputes, reducing the likelihood of armed conflicts.

Global Solidarity: Multilateralism promotes global solidarity and cooperation by recognizing the interdependence of nations and the shared nature of global challenges. It encourages collaboration and mutual support to address issues that transcend national boundaries, such as climate change, pandemics, and poverty.

III. Key Institutions and Mechanisms

Multilateralism finds expression through various institutions and mechanisms that facilitate international cooperation. These institutions play a pivotal role in shaping global governance and addressing a wide range of issues. Some key institutions include:

United Nations (UN): The UN is the most prominent multilateral organization, composed of 193 member states. It serves as a platform for member states to address pressing global issues, such as peace and security, development, human rights, and climate change. The UN General Assembly, Security Council, and specialized agencies work together to foster collaboration and address global challenges.

World Trade Organization (WTO): The WTO is an international organization that regulates global trade and promotes the liberalization of international commerce. It provides a forum for member states to negotiate trade agreements, resolve trade disputes, and establish rules and standards for global trade. The WTO plays a crucial role in facilitating multilateral trade negotiations and ensuring a level playing field for all member states.

International Monetary Fund (IMF): **The IMF is an** organization that promotes global financial stability and facilitates cooperation in monetary matters. It provides financial assistance, policy advice, and technical assistance to member countries facing economic challenges. The IMF fosters multilateral economic cooperation by promoting sound economic policies and facilitating the exchange of information and expertise among member states.

World Bank: **The World Bank is a** multilateral development institution that provides financial and technical assistance to developing countries. It aims to reduce poverty, promote sustainable development, and address global challenges such as climate change and inequality. The World Bank supports multilateralism by channeling resources and expertise to countries in need and fostering collaboration among governments, civil society, and the private sector.

: In addition to global institutions, regional organizations also play a significant role in promoting multilateralism. Examples include the European Union (EU), African Union (AU), Association of Southeast Asian Nations (ASEAN), and Organization of American States (OAS). These regional bodies facilitate cooperation, integration, and collective decision-making among member states, addressing regional challenges and promoting multilateral approaches to global issues.

IV. Benefits of Multilateralism

Multilateralism offers numerous benefits that make it a crucial framework for global cooperation:

Collective Problem-Solving: Multilateralism allows nations to pool resources, expertise, and perspectives to tackle complex global challenges effectively. By involving multiple stakeholders, multilateral approaches can generate more comprehensive and innovative solutions that take into account diverse interests and perspectives.

Increased Legitimacy and Credibility: Multilateralism enhances the legitimacy and credibility of global actions and decisions. Agreements reached through multilateral negotiations carry greater weight and are more widely accepted, as they involve a broader range of voices and perspectives.

Peace and Stability: Multilateralism promotes peaceful conflict resolution by providing platforms for dialogue, negotiation, and mediation. By encouraging peaceful means of resolving disputes, it reduces the likelihood of armed conflicts and contributes to global peace and stability.

Global Economic Growth: Multilateral trade agreements, facilitated by institutions like the WTO, contribute to global economic growth by reducing trade barriers and promoting a rules-based trading system. This fosters economic interdependence, increases market access for all member states, and stimulates investment and job creation.

Collective Security: Multilateralism, as exemplified by the United Nations Security Council, plays a crucial role in maintaining international peace and security. By providing a forum for diplomatic engagement and collective action, it helps prevent conflicts, promotes disarmament, and coordinates peacekeeping efforts.

V. Challenges and Criticisms of Multilateralism

Despite its benefits, multilateralism also faces challenges and criticisms that require attention and continuous improvement:

Power Imbalances: Power imbalances among member states can hinder the effectiveness of multilateral institutions. Powerful nations may exert undue influence, while the voices of smaller and less influential countries can be marginalized. Addressing these imbalances is crucial to ensure a more equitable and inclusive multilateral system.

Slow Decision-Making: The multilateral decision-making process can be slow and cumbersome due to the need for consensus among diverse stakeholders. This can delay timely action on pressing issues and make it challenging to respond effectively to rapidly evolving crises.

Non-Compliance and Enforcement: Multilateral agreements and resolutions are only effective if member states comply with them. However, enforcement mechanisms for non-compliance can be limited, leading to challenges in upholding the commitments made under multilateral frameworks. Strengthening compliance mechanisms and ensuring accountability is essential to maintain the integrity of multilateralism.

Divergent Interests: Member states often have divergent interests and priorities, making it challenging to reach consensus on critical issues. Negotiations can be complex and protracted, requiring compromises and trade-offs that may not fully satisfy all parties involved.

Lack of Representation: Multilateral institutions may not adequately represent the diversity of the global community. The inclusion of marginalized voices, such as developing countries, small island states, and indigenous communities, is crucial to ensure that multilateral decisions and policies consider the needs and perspectives of all stakeholders.

Rise of Unilateralism and Protectionism: The rise of unilateralism and protectionist tendencies in some countries poses a challenge to multilateralism. These actions can undermine global cooperation, disrupt trade relations, and hinder the achievement of shared objectives.

VI. The Relevance of Multilateralism in a Changing World

In an increasingly interconnected and complex world, multilateralism remains highly relevant and necessary. Several factors highlight its ongoing importance:

Global Challenges: Global challenges, such as climate change, public health crises, poverty, inequality, and terrorism, require collective action and cooperation among nations. Multilateralism provides a platform to address these challenges comprehensively, mobilize resources, and develop coordinated strategies for their resolution.

Interconnectedness: The world is more interconnected than ever before, with economic, social, and environmental issues transcending national borders. Multilateral approaches enable the coordination and harmonization of policies, standards, and regulations to address common issues effectively.

Sustainable Development Goals: The United Nations' Sustainable Development Goals (SDGs) provide a comprehensive framework for global development. Achieving these goals necessitates international cooperation, resource mobilization, and policy coordination, all of which are facilitated by multilateralism.

Technology and Innovation: Rapid technological advancements and innovations have transformed the global landscape. Multilateralism can facilitate the sharing of technological expertise, promote ethical standards, and address potential challenges and risks associated with emerging technologies.

Peace and Security: Multilateralism remains crucial in maintaining international peace and security. Collective security mechanisms, peacekeeping operations, and disarmament efforts require the cooperation and collaboration of multiple nations.

Human Rights and Social Justice: Multilateralism plays a vital role in promoting and protecting human rights, fostering social justice, and ensuring the inclusion and empowerment of marginalized groups. Multilateral institutions provide platforms for dialogue, accountability, and advocacy in these areas.

The concept of multilateralism represents a crucial framework for global cooperation, problem-solving, and governance. Through its principles of sovereign equality, collective decision-making, rule of law, peaceful conflict resolution, and global solidarity, multilateralism fosters collaboration among nations to address pressing global challenges.

Despite the challenges it faces, multilateralism offers significant benefits, including collective problem-solving, increased legitimacy, peace and stability, economic growth, and collective security. In a rapidly changing world characterized by interconnectedness and complex challenges, multilateralism remains highly relevant.

Efforts to strengthen multilateral institutions, address power imbalances, enhance compliance mechanisms, and ensure representation are essential to realize the full potential of multilateralism. By embracing the principles of multilateralism and working together, nations can foster a sustainable future for all, where global challenges are effectively addressed, peace and security are upheld, and human rights and social justice are safeguarded.

Chinese Foreign Policy Priorities

An Introduction,China, as one of the world's major powers, has witnessed significant transformations in its foreign policy priorities over the years. From a traditionally isolationist approach to its current proactive and assertive stance, Chinese foreign policy has evolved to reflect its rising global influence and economic prowess. This introduction aims to provide a comprehensive overview of China's foreign policy priorities, highlighting key elements and developments that shape its international engagement. By examining China's historical context, core principles, regional and global interests, and evolving challenges, we can gain a deeper understanding of China's approach to international relations and its significance for the global order.

Historical Context

To understand China's foreign policy priorities, it is crucial to consider its historical context. China has a rich history spanning thousands of years, characterized by periods of imperial dominance, isolation, and ideological shifts. The Opium Wars and the subsequent "Century of Humiliation" (1840-1949) deeply influenced China's perception of the world and its determination to regain its national dignity and status. The Chinese Communist Party's (CCP) rise to power in 1949 marked a turning point, as China embarked on a path of socialist revolution and sought to establish itself as a global leader of the developing world.

Core Principles

China's foreign policy is guided by a set of core principles that shape its approach to international relations. These principles include:

2.1. Non-Interference: China adheres to the principle of non-interference in the internal affairs of other states. This principle stems from its historical experience of foreign interference and a commitment to respect state sovereignty.

2.2. Peaceful Development: China emphasizes the pursuit of peaceful development, focusing on economic growth, social stability, and regional cooperation. It aims to maintain a peaceful international environment conducive to its economic transformation and social progress.

2.3. Harmonious World: The concept of a "harmonious world" underlies China's foreign policy vision. It envisions a global order based on equality, mutual respect, and win-win cooperation, challenging the dominance of Western-centric ideologies.

Regional Interests

China's foreign policy priorities are strongly influenced by its regional interests, particularly in East Asia. Key factors shaping China's regional approach include:

3.1. Taiwan: The issue of Taiwan remains a core concern for China's foreign policy. Beijing considers Taiwan an integral part of its territory and seeks to prevent its international recognition as an independent state.

3.2. South China Sea: China's territorial claims and assertive actions in the South China Sea have drawn international attention. China's pursuit of maritime control in this strategic region is driven by its economic and security interests, as well as its desire to project power in the Asia-Pacific.

3.3. North Korea: China's approach to North Korea is influenced by a combination of factors, including historical ties, regional stability, and concerns about potential refugee crises and nuclear proliferation. China seeks to maintain stability on the Korean Peninsula and influence North Korea's behavior through diplomatic means.

Global Interests

China's foreign policy priorities also extend beyond its immediate region to encompass global interests. These global interests are driven by economic considerations, energy security, diplomatic influence, and the pursuit of a multipolar world order. Key elements of China's global engagement include:

4.1. Belt and Road Initiative (BRI): Launched in 2013, the BRI is a flagship foreign policy initiative aimed at promoting connectivity, infrastructure development, and economic cooperation across Asia, Europe, Africa, and beyond. It serves China's economic interests by expanding its markets, securing access to resources, and enhancing its geopolitical influence.

4.2. Multilateralism: China increasingly emphasizes multilateralism as a means to promote global governance and advance its interests. China has actively sought to strengthen its participation in multilateral institutions such as the United Nations, World Trade Organization, and Asian Infrastructure Investment Bank. It also champions initiatives like the Shanghai Cooperation Organization and the BRICS (Brazil, Russia, India, China, South Africa) grouping to foster cooperation among emerging economies.

4.3. Climate Change and Sustainable Development: Recognizing the importance of global environmental challenges, China has positioned itself as a leader in combating climate change and promoting sustainable development. It has made significant commitments to reduce greenhouse gas emissions, invest in renewable energy, and participate in international climate negotiations.

4.4. Economic Diplomacy: China's economic growth and global integration have made economic diplomacy a vital aspect of its foreign policy. It actively engages in trade negotiations, investment agreements, and economic partnerships to expand its market access, secure resources, and promote its industries abroad.

Evolving Challenges

China's foreign policy priorities are not without challenges. Several factors complicate China's pursuit of its objectives and shape its decision-making process:

5.1. Geopolitical Competition: China's rise as a global power has led to increased geopolitical competition, particularly with the United States. The U.S.-China relationship is characterized by strategic rivalry, trade disputes, and conflicting visions of international order. Managing this complex relationship and avoiding an escalation of tensions is a significant challenge for China's foreign policy.

5.2. Human Rights Concerns: China's human rights record, particularly regarding issues such as religious freedom, freedom of expression, and ethnic minority rights, has drawn criticism from the international community. Balancing its pursuit of national interests with international norms and human rights concerns presents a challenge for China's foreign policy.

5.3. Regional Power Dynamics: China's growing influence in the Asia-Pacific region has raised concerns among neighboring countries, leading to tensions over territorial disputes, military build-up, and historical grievances. Navigating these complex dynamics while maintaining regional stability poses a challenge for China's foreign policy.

5.4. Technological Competition: As technology increasingly shapes global politics and security, China's pursuit of technological advancement and dominance, particularly in areas such as 5G, artificial intelligence, and cybersecurity, has raised concerns about data privacy, intellectual property theft, and potential military applications.

China's foreign policy priorities reflect its status as a rising global power with a unique historical and ideological background. Guided by core principles such as non-interference, peaceful development, and the vision of a harmonious world, China seeks to protect its regional interests, expand its global influence, and promote a multipolar international order. However, challenges such as geopolitical competition, human rights concerns, regional power dynamics, and technological competition pose significant tests to China's foreign policy approach. Understanding China's foreign policy priorities is crucial for comprehending its role in global affairs and predicting its future trajectory in an increasingly complex and interconnected world.

Part I: Historical Context

The rise of China as a global power has had a profound impact on the international system. As China's economic and military capabilities have grown, it has sought to shape the global order according to its interests and values. A crucial aspect of China's international relations (IR) strategy has been its engagement with multilateralism. China's approach to multilateralism has evolved over time, reflecting its historical context, domestic priorities, and changing global dynamics.

This paper aims to provide a comprehensive analysis of the historical context of Chinese IR strategy for multilateralism. By examining key historical events, policy shifts, and ideological influences, we can gain a deeper understanding of China's approach to multilateral institutions and its broader foreign policy objectives.

Pre-1949: The Legacy of Chinese Civilization

To understand China's approach to multilateralism, it is essential to consider the historical legacy of Chinese civilization. China has a long history of engaging with the world through diplomatic and economic interactions. Throughout the centuries, China's interactions with neighboring states and distant civilizations influenced its diplomatic practices and perceptions of international order.

Chinese civilization, characterized by the tributary system, emphasized hierarchical relations between China and its neighboring states. China was considered the central power, and other countries paid tribute to gain access to Chinese trade and cultural benefits. This historical experience shaped China's perception of its place in the international order and its preference for stability and continuity.

1949-1978: The Foundational Years of the People's Republic of China

The establishment of the People's Republic of China (PRC) in 1949 marked a turning point in China's foreign policy. The early years of the PRC were characterized by a revolutionary zeal and a focus on consolidating power domestically. During this period, China adopted a revolutionary foreign policy posture, emphasizing anti-imperialism and support for national liberation movements.

China's engagement with multilateralism during this period was limited. The Chinese leadership was critical of existing multilateral institutions, perceiving them as dominated by Western powers. Instead, China focused on building alliances with socialist countries and leading the non-aligned movement. The 1955 Bandung Conference, where China played a prominent role, marked an important milestone in China's engagement with multilateralism and its pursuit of collective security.

1978-1992: Deng Xiaoping's Reform and Opening-Up

The period from 1978 to 1992 witnessed a significant shift in China's domestic and foreign policy under the leadership of Deng Xiaoping. Deng introduced a series of economic reforms that opened up China to the world and transformed its economic landscape. This period also saw a gradual shift in China's approach to multilateralism.

Deng Xiaoping's strategy can be characterized as "hide your strength and bide your time." China focused on economic development and sought a stable international environment to support its modernization efforts. As a result, China started to engage more actively with existing multilateral institutions such as the United Nations (UN) and World Trade Organization (WTO).

1992-2002: The Era of Jiang Zemin and Zhu Rongji
The era of Jiang Zemin and Zhu Rongji witnessed China's increasing integration into the global economy and its pursuit of a "peaceful rise" strategy. China actively sought to join international

organizations and promote its economic interests through multilateral mechanisms. Jiang Zemin's concept of the "Three Represents" emphasized the importance of the Communist Party maintaining close ties with all social classes, including entrepreneurs and intellectuals.

China's engagement with multilateralism during this period focused primarily on economic issues. It actively participated in regional organizations such as the Asia-Pacific Economic Cooperation (APEC) and played a prominent role in negotiations for the establishment of the World Trade Organization (WTO). China's accession to the WTO in 2001 marked a significant milestone in its integration into the global trading system.

2002-2012: Hu Jintao's Harmonious World
Under the leadership of Hu Jintao, China's foreign policy rhetoric shifted towards the concept of a "harmonious world." The notion of a harmonious world emphasized peaceful coexistence, mutual

respect, and win-win cooperation. China sought to strengthen its role in global governance by advocating for the reform of existing international institutions to better reflect the interests of developing countries.

During this period, China's engagement with multilateralism expanded beyond economic issues. It actively participated in forums such as the United Nations Security Council (UNSC) and the G20, where it sought to promote its vision of a multipolar world order and enhance its influence on global affairs.

2012-Present: Xi Jinping's Vision for a Community with a Shared Future for Mankind

Since assuming power in 2012, President Xi Jinping has articulated a comprehensive vision for China's role in the world. Xi's foreign policy concept of a "community with a shared future for mankind" highlights the importance of cooperation, inclusiveness, and mutual benefit in international relations. It reflects China's aspiration to shape global governance institutions and promote its interests within a more multipolar and equitable international order.

Under Xi's leadership, China has taken a more assertive stance on the global stage. It has launched ambitious initiatives such as the Belt and Road Initiative (BRI), which aims to promote connectivity, infrastructure development, and economic cooperation across regions. China has also sought to play a more active role in international organizations, such as the World Health Organization (WHO) and the International Monetary Fund (IMF).

China's engagement with multilateralism under Xi Jinping has faced both praise and criticism. While some view China's increased involvement in global governance as a positive contribution to addressing global challenges, others express concerns about

China's intentions and its impact on the existing international order.

The historical context of China's IR strategy for multilateralism provides valuable insights into its evolving approach to global governance. From the legacy of Chinese civilization to the revolutionary zeal of the early years of the PRC, and from Deng Xiaoping's reform and opening-up to Xi Jinping's vision for a shared future, China's engagement with multilateralism has been shaped by a combination of historical experiences, domestic priorities, and shifting global dynamics.

China's strategy for multilateralism has evolved from a focus on ideological alignment and support for national liberation movements to a more pragmatic approach centered around economic development and global influence. As China's economic and military capabilities have grown, so too has its ambition to shape the rules and institutions of the international system.

Understanding China's historical context is crucial for comprehending its current and future approach to multilateralism. It helps to decipher China's motivations, interests, and potential areas of cooperation or contention with other nations. As China continues to play an increasingly influential role in global affairs, its engagement with multilateralism will continue to be a subject of critical importance for international relations scholars, policymakers, and practitioners alike.

Historical Evolution of Chinese IR Strategy

The study of International Relations (IR) involves understanding how states interact with each other in the global arena, pursuing their national interests, and employing strategies to ensure their security and promote their influence. China, with its rich history and global significance, has been a key player in international affairs for centuries. The evolution of Chinese IR strategy offers valuable insights into its diplomatic, economic, and military pursuits, and sheds light on its rise as a major global power in the modern era.

Chinese IR strategy has been shaped by a multitude of factors, including its geographic location, historical experiences, cultural values, and evolving domestic and international dynamics. This essay aims to provide a comprehensive overview of the historical evolution of Chinese IR strategy, highlighting key periods and themes that have shaped its approach to international affairs.

Early Dynasties and the Tributary System
China's early dynasties, such as the Qin, Han, Tang, and Ming, laid the foundation for its approach to IR. During these periods, China saw itself as the central civilization, a self-proclaimed "Middle Kingdom," surrounded by peripheral states. The tributary system, a hierarchical structure of international relations, emerged as a dominant feature of China's engagement with its neighbors.

Under the tributary system, states paid tribute to the Chinese emperor, recognizing China's cultural superiority and seeking its protection and favor. China, in turn, granted trade privileges and occasionally military protection to its tributary states. This strategy allowed China to maintain a degree of regional hegemony and secure its borders, reinforcing its self-perception as the central power in East Asia.

The Century of Humiliation and Self-Strengthening Movements

The 19th century marked a significant turning point in Chinese IR strategy. This period, often referred to as the "Century of Humiliation," saw China suffer military defeats, territorial losses, and economic exploitation at the hands of Western powers and Japan. These experiences shattered China's self-perception as the dominant power and exposed the weaknesses of its traditional strategy.

In response, Chinese intellectuals and statesmen initiated self-strengthening movements, advocating for modernization and reforms to restore China's strength and sovereignty. Scholars like Liang Qichao and Kang Youwei called for a reinterpretation of Chinese traditions and the adoption of Western knowledge and technology to catch up with the Western powers.

Maoist Era and Revolutionary Diplomacy

The establishment of the People's Republic of China (PRC) in 1949 marked a radical shift in Chinese IR strategy. Mao Zedong, the founding father of the PRC, pursued a revolutionary and ideologically driven approach to international relations. Mao sought to spread communism and support revolutionary movements worldwide, challenging the existing global order dominated by Western powers.

During the Cold War, China aligned itself with the Soviet Union against the United States, advocating for anti-imperialism and supporting communist insurgencies in Southeast Asia, Africa, and Latin America. Mao's foreign policy was characterized by a mix of revolutionary diplomacy, asymmetric warfare, and a desire to maintain strategic autonomy.

Deng Xiaoping's Reform and Opening Up
In the late 1970s, Deng Xiaoping came to power and initiated a period of economic reform and opening up. This transformative era reshaped China's approach to international relations. Deng emphasized economic development as the top priority, recognizing that a prosperous and stable China would enhance its global influence.

Deng's strategy included attracting foreign investment, establishing Special Economic Zones, and pursuing a policy of "peaceful rise." China actively sought to integrate into the global economy, join international organizations, and pursue diplomatic normalization with other countries. This pragmatic approach facilitated China's economic rise and paved the way for its subsequent emergence as a major global Peaceful Development and Harmonious World.

Under the leadership of Jiang Zemin and further advanced by Hu Jintao, China articulated its foreign policy approach as one of "peaceful development" and "building a harmonious world." This strategy aimed to address concerns about China's rise and reassure the international community of its peaceful intentions.

The concept of peaceful development emphasized China's commitment to economic growth, domestic stability, and cooperation with other nations. China sought to become a responsible stakeholder in the international system, promoting multilateralism, and participating in global governance initiatives.

The notion of a harmonious world emphasized the importance of mutual respect, equality, and win-win cooperation in international relations. China advocated for a multipolar world order, challenging the dominance of Western powers and advocating for a more equitable global system.

Xi Jinping's Era and the Belt and Road Initiative

Since assuming power in 2012, President Xi Jinping has introduced a series of new initiatives that have shaped China's contemporary IR strategy. The most significant among them is the Belt and Road Initiative (BRI), a massive infrastructure and economic development project aiming to enhance connectivity between China and countries across Asia, Europe, Africa, and beyond.

The BRI reflects China's aspiration to extend its economic influence and build stronger ties with other nations. It has both economic and strategic dimensions, promoting trade, investment, and infrastructure development, while also expanding China's geopolitical influence and fostering diplomatic relationships.

Additionally, Xi Jinping's administration has adopted a more assertive and confident approach to foreign policy, particularly in territorial disputes in the South China Sea and the East China Sea. China has pursued a policy of territorial consolidation, asserting its claims and challenging the regional status quo.

The historical evolution of Chinese IR strategy demonstrates the complex interplay between China's domestic transformation and its engagement with the international system. From the tributary system of ancient dynasties to the revolutionary diplomacy of Mao Zedong, and from Deng Xiaoping's economic reforms to Xi Jinping's Belt and Road Initiative, China's approach to international relations has constantly adapted to its changing circumstances and aspirations.

China's rise as a major global power has presented both opportunities and challenges for the international community. Its evolving IR strategy reflects a mix of continuity and innovation, drawing on traditional cultural values, historical experiences, and contemporary geopolitical realities.

Understanding the historical evolution of Chinese IR strategy is essential for comprehending China's motivations, aspirations, and behavior in the international arena. It provides insights into how China perceives its role as a global power, how it seeks to protect its national interests, and how it navigates its relationships with other states.

As China continues to assert itself on the global stage, it is crucial for policymakers, scholars, and practitioners to analyze and engage with China's evolving IR strategy. By promoting dialogue, cooperation, and mutual understanding, the international community can work towards a more stable and prosperous world order in which China's rise can be accommodated and harnessed for the collective benefit of all.

Traditional Chinese Foreign Policy Principles

Traditional Chinese foreign policy principles have shaped China's approach to international relations for centuries. Deeply rooted in Chinese history, culture, and philosophy, these principles provide insights into the country's strategic thinking and its pursuit of national interests in the global arena. By understanding these principles, one can gain valuable perspectives on China's diplomatic strategies, regional aspirations, and engagement with the international community.

China's foreign policy principles have evolved over time, reflecting historical, geopolitical, and ideological shifts. From the early days of the Zhou Dynasty to the modern era, Chinese foreign policy has been guided by key concepts such as sovereignty, non-interference, harmony, and peaceful coexistence. These principles continue to influence China's diplomatic engagements and its interactions with other nations.

This essay aims to explore the traditional Chinese foreign policy principles that have shaped China's role in international relations. It will examine the historical context and philosophical foundations of these principles, and their application in contemporary Chinese foreign policy. By delving into these principles, we can gain a deeper understanding of China's worldview and its evolving role in the global order.

Historical Context:

The principles that underpin China's foreign policy have deep historical roots. China's long history of centralized governance and imperial rule has had a profound impact on its approach to foreign relations. The concept of the "Mandate of Heaven" provided legitimacy to the ruling dynasty and shaped China's interactions with neighboring states. The tributary system, which governed China's relations with other East Asian states, was based on the belief in China's cultural and political superiority.

During the period of colonial expansion and imperialist encroachment, China faced numerous challenges to its sovereignty and territorial integrity. These experiences shaped China's determination to safeguard its national interests and maintain its independence in the face of external pressures. The "Century of Humiliation" (mid-19th to mid-20th century) left a lasting imprint on China's foreign policy thinking, emphasizing the need for self-reliance, national rejuvenation, and protection of its core interests.

Philosophical Foundations:

Chinese foreign policy principles are deeply influenced by traditional philosophical systems, notably Confucianism, Taoism, and Legalism. Confucianism emphasizes social order, hierarchy, and harmony in human relationships, which extends to international relations as well. The Confucian concept of "All-Under-Heaven" promotes the idea of a universal order where China occupies a central position as the moral and cultural exemplar.

Taoism, on the other hand, emphasizes the pursuit of balance, non-action, and adaptation to natural rhythms. This philosophy encourages flexibility and pragmatism in foreign policy, as well as the avoidance of unnecessary conflict. Legalism, with its focus on strict governance and the rule of law, has also influenced China's approach to domestic and international affairs, emphasizing the importance of stability and order.

Core Principles:

a) Sovereignty: China places a high value on territorial integrity and national sovereignty. The historical experiences of foreign invasions and territorial concessions have reinforced China's commitment to maintaining its territorial boundaries and resisting external interference in its internal affairs. The principle of sovereignty is seen as a cornerstone of China's foreign policy, and any attempts to challenge or undermine it are met with resistance.

b) Non-interference: China adheres to the principle of non-interference in the internal affairs of other countries. This principle is rooted in the concept of respecting the sovereignty and independence of other nations, as well as the principle of reciprocity. China emphasizes mutual respect and equality in its relations with other countries, advocating for a multipolar world order where each nation has the right to determine its own political, economic, and social systems without external interference.

c) Harmony and Peaceful Coexistence: The principle of harmony is another key aspect of traditional Chinese foreign policy. This principle emphasizes the importance of building and maintaining friendly relations with other countries, based on mutual respect, understanding, and cooperation. China's focus on peaceful coexistence stems from its belief that conflict and confrontation should be avoided, and that differences between nations can be resolved through dialogue and negotiation.

d) Mutual Benefit: The principle of mutual benefit is also central to China's foreign policy. This principle stresses the importance of building mutually beneficial relationships with other countries, where each party gains from the interaction. China sees international cooperation and economic integration as key components of achieving this goal, and has actively pursued trade and investment partnerships with other countries to advance its economic interests.

e) Diplomacy: Diplomacy is an essential tool in China's foreign policy toolkit. China places great emphasis on diplomacy as a means of advancing its interests, promoting its values, and building relationships with other countries. Diplomatic engagements take place at multiple levels, from high-level government-to-government interactions to people-to-people exchanges and cultural diplomacy. China's diplomatic efforts aim to promote stability, peace, and cooperation in the international system.

Contemporary Application:

China's traditional foreign policy principles continue to guide its approach to international relations in the contemporary era. In recent years, China has sought to strengthen its global standing and pursue its strategic interests through a range of diplomatic, economic, and military measures. While China remains committed to its core principles, it has also adapted its approach to reflect changing global realities.

a) Sovereignty: China's commitment to sovereignty and territorial integrity remains a fundamental aspect of its foreign policy. China has been particularly assertive in its territorial claims in the South China Sea, where it has built and militarized artificial islands to bolster its claims to disputed areas. China has also been critical of any perceived threats to its sovereignty, including the US policy of "freedom of navigation" operations in the region.

b) Non-interference: China's adherence to the principle of non-interference remains a key aspect of its foreign policy. However, China's growing global footprint and economic interests have led it to become more involved in the affairs of other countries. China's "Belt and Road Initiative" (BRI), for example, has seen it invest in infrastructure projects in numerous countries, raising concerns among some about China's growing influence and potential for political interference.

c) Harmony and Peaceful Coexistence: China's focus on harmony and peaceful coexistence continues to shape its foreign policy approach. China has sought to build relationships with other countries through diplomacy and economic cooperation, and has worked to resolve disputes through dialogue and negotiation. However, China's growing assertiveness in the region and its military buildup have raised concerns among some about its commitment to peaceful coexistence.

d) Mutual Benefit: China's pursuit of mutual benefit remains a key driver of its foreign policy. China has sought to build economic relationships with other countries, through initiatives such as the BRI, as a means of advancing its interests and promoting global economic integration. However, concerns have been raised about the impact of China's economic influence on other countries, including its potential for debt-trap diplomacy and predatory lending practices.

e) Diplomacy: China's emphasis on diplomacy remains an important aspect of its foreign policy. China has sought to build relationships with other countries through high-level government-to-government interactions, as well as people-to-people exchanges and cultural diplomacy. China's diplomatic efforts have helped it to build relationships with countries around the world, and have helped to promote its values and interests.

China's traditional foreign policy principles have played a central role in shaping its approach to international relations over the centuries. These principles, rooted in Chinese history, culture, and philosophy, provide valuable insights into China's strategic thinking and its pursuit of national interests in the global arena.

The historical context of Chinese foreign policy, marked by experiences of invasion, territorial concessions, and the "Century of Humiliation," has deeply influenced China's determination to safeguard its sovereignty and national interests. The philosophical foundations of Confucianism, Taoism, and Legalism have shaped China's worldview and its approach to international relations. Confucianism's emphasis on social order and hierarchy, Taoism's focus on balance and non-action, and Legalism's emphasis on governance and stability have all contributed to the formulation of China's foreign policy principles.

The core principles of Chinese foreign policy, including sovereignty, non-interference, harmony, peaceful coexistence, and mutual benefit, continue to guide China's diplomatic engagements and interactions with other nations. China places a high value on territorial integrity and national sovereignty, as a result of its historical experiences. The principle of non-interference reflects China's belief in respecting the sovereignty and independence of other nations, while emphasizing mutual respect and equality in international relations.

Harmony and peaceful coexistence are central to China's foreign policy approach, emphasizing the importance of friendly relations, dialogue, and cooperation with other countries. China seeks to build mutually beneficial relationships, where each party gains from the interaction. Diplomacy plays a crucial role in China's foreign policy, serving as a means to advance its interests, promote stability, and build relationships with other countries.

In contemporary times, China's traditional foreign policy principles continue to shape its approach to international relations, albeit with adaptations to changing global dynamics. China remains committed to safeguarding its sovereignty and territorial integrity, as evidenced by its assertiveness in territorial disputes. While adhering to the principle of non-interference, China's growing global influence and economic interests have led to increased involvement in the affairs of other countries, raising concerns about its intentions.

China's focus on harmony and peaceful coexistence is reflected in its diplomatic engagements and efforts to resolve disputes through dialogue and negotiation. However, its military buildup and assertiveness in certain regions have raised questions about its commitment to peaceful coexistence.

China's pursuit of mutual benefit remains a driving force in its foreign policy, as seen in its economic initiatives such as the Belt and Road Initiative. While aiming to advance its own interests, China's economic influence and practices have raised concerns about potential negative impacts on other countries.

Diplomacy continues to be a key tool in China's foreign policy, enabling it to build relationships, promote its values, and advance its interests. China's diplomatic efforts have helped it establish connections with countries around the world, contributing to its global standing.

In conclusion, traditional Chinese foreign policy principles have played a significant role in shaping China's approach to international relations. These principles, deeply rooted in Chinese history, culture, and philosophy, have influenced China's strategic thinking, regional aspirations, and engagement with the international community. Understanding these principles provides valuable insights into China's worldview and its evolving role in the global order. As China continues to assert its presence on the world stage, an awareness of its traditional foreign policy principles is crucial for comprehending its actions and aspirations in the international arena.

Maoist Era and Isolationism

The Maoist era and isolationism in China refer to a period of the country's history when the Chinese Communist Party (CCP) under the leadership of Mao Zedong pursued a policy of self-reliance and isolation from the rest of the world. This period, which lasted from the mid-1940s to the late 1970s, was characterized by various political, economic, and social policies that aimed to transform China into a socialist country and promote its development.

During this era, China underwent significant changes in its political, economic, and social systems. The CCP implemented various policies to achieve its goals of socialist transformation and self-reliance, such as collectivization of agriculture, industrialization, and the suppression of dissent. These policies resulted in both positive and negative outcomes, shaping China's trajectory for decades to come.

One of the main reasons for the CCP's adoption of isolationist policies was its desire to consolidate power and maintain control over the country. The CCP had emerged victorious from a long and bloody civil war with the Nationalist government, and it saw isolationism as a way to safeguard its power and legitimacy. By promoting self-reliance, the CCP aimed to reduce dependence on foreign powers and create a socialist economy that was free from capitalist influence.

The Maoist era was marked by several key policies and initiatives that aimed to promote self-reliance and socialist transformation. One of the most significant was the Great Leap Forward, which began in 1958 and aimed to transform China's economy through rapid industrialization and agricultural collectivization. The Great Leap Forward involved the mobilization of millions of peasants into communes, the establishment of backyard steel furnaces, and the promotion of communal dining. However, the policies resulted in widespread famine and economic collapse, leading to the deaths of millions of people.

Another significant policy during the Maoist era was the Cultural Revolution, which began in 1966 and lasted for a decade. The Cultural Revolution aimed to promote Maoist ideology and suppress dissent within the CCP and broader society. The policies resulted in the persecution of intellectuals, artists, and other perceived enemies of the state, leading to widespread violence and social upheaval.

Despite the negative outcomes of these policies, the Maoist era also saw significant progress in certain areas. For example, the period saw significant improvements in literacy rates, healthcare, and infrastructure development. Additionally, China's military capabilities expanded significantly during this period, making it a major player on the global stage.

However, the isolationist policies of the Maoist era also had significant implications for China's relations with the rest of the world. China's self-reliance policies meant that it had limited trade and diplomatic relations with other countries. This led to the country's isolation from the international community and a lack of exposure to new ideas and technologies. As a result, China's economy and industries lagged behind those of other countries, and its citizens had limited access to foreign goods and cultural influences.

The Maoist era and isolationism in China came to an end in the late 1970s, when Deng Xiaoping became the country's leader and initiated a series of economic reforms that opened China to the world. These reforms, known as the "Four Modernizations," aimed to promote economic development and modernization by embracing foreign investment and technology. The reforms led to significant changes in China's economic and social systems and propelled the country to become one of the world's fastest-growing economies.

In conclusion, the Maoist era and isolationism in China represent a significant period in the country's history. The policies of the era aimed to promote self-reliance and socialist transformation but had significant negative outcomes, such as economic collapse, social upheaval, and isolation from the rest of the world. Despite these outcomes, the era also saw significant progress in certain areas, such as improvements in literacy rates, healthcare, and infrastructure development. The Maoist era also strengthened China's military capabilities, establishing it as a major global player. However, the isolationist policies limited China's trade and diplomatic relations, resulting in a lack of exposure to new ideas and technologies, and hindering economic growth and cultural exchange.

The end of the Maoist era and the subsequent opening up of China under Deng Xiaoping's leadership marked a turning point in the country's history. Deng's economic reforms aimed to modernize China's economy and integrate it into the global market. The Four Modernizations focused on agriculture, industry, national defense, and science and technology, laying the foundation for China's rapid economic growth in the following decades.

The transition from isolationism to a more open and internationally engaged China brought about significant changes. China embraced foreign investment, established special economic zones, and implemented policies to attract foreign businesses. These measures contributed to the growth of China's manufacturing sector and export industry, transforming it into the world's largest exporter and second-largest economy.

China's engagement with the global community also expanded in the realms of diplomacy, culture, and education. The country became an active participant in international organizations and forged diplomatic ties with numerous nations. It also embraced cultural exchange and welcomed foreign influences, leading to a flourishing of arts, entertainment, and the exchange of ideas.

The shift away from isolationism had profound implications for China's society and people. The economic reforms lifted millions of Chinese citizens out of poverty and contributed to an overall improvement in living standards. With increased exposure to the outside world, Chinese citizens gained access to a wider range of goods, information, and opportunities. The rapid growth of China's middle class created a consumer market that attracted multinational corporations, further driving economic development.

The end of isolationism also prompted a reevaluation of China's place in the international arena. As China became an economic powerhouse, it sought to assert its influence on regional and global affairs. This was evident in its "Going Out" policy, which encouraged Chinese businesses to invest abroad and promote China's economic interests overseas. Additionally, China embarked on ambitious infrastructure projects such as the Belt and Road Initiative, which aimed to enhance connectivity and trade with countries across Asia, Europe, and Africa.

While China's opening up brought about numerous benefits, it also posed challenges and complexities. The rapid economic growth led to environmental concerns, social inequality, and an increasing demand for resources. China's rise as a global power also raised geopolitical tensions and prompted debates over issues such as human rights, intellectual property rights, and trade imbalances.

In recent years, China has faced scrutiny over its domestic policies, including issues related to human rights, censorship, and political repression.

These challenges have generated debates and discussions both within China and among the international community. As China continues to grow economically and assert itself globally, questions arise about the balance between its aspirations for global leadership and the expectations and values of the international community.

In conclusion, the Maoist era and China's period of isolationism represented a significant chapter in the country's history. The policies pursued during this time aimed to promote self-reliance and transform China into a socialist nation but had mixed results. While there were achievements in areas such as literacy rates and infrastructure development, the isolationist policies limited China's engagement with the rest of the world, hindering economic growth and cultural exchange.

The subsequent shift away from isolationism under Deng Xiaoping's leadership brought about profound changes, with economic reforms leading to rapid growth and China's emergence as a major global power. China's engagement with the international community expanded, opening avenues for trade, diplomacy, and cultural exchange. However, this transformation also presented challenges, including environmental concerns, social inequality, and geopolitical tensions.

As China continues to navigate its role in the global arena, it faces ongoing scrutiny and debates about its domestic policies and its aspirations for global leadership. The balance between China's desire for economic development, political control, and adherence to international norms and values remains a topic of discussion both within the country and among its international counterparts.

China's evolution from the Maoist era and isolationism to its current position as a global player has had far-reaching implications not only for China itself but also for the rest of the world. Economically, China's integration into the global market has created opportunities for trade and investment, but it has also disrupted global supply chains and raised concerns about fair competition and intellectual property rights. Politically, China's rise has shifted the geopolitical landscape, influencing regional dynamics and challenging established norms and institutions.

China's foreign policy has evolved as it seeks to balance its economic interests with its strategic goals. The Belt and Road Initiative, for example, has been seen by some as an effort to expand China's influence and secure access to resources, while others view it as a means to foster regional development and connectivity. China's military modernization has also raised concerns among neighboring countries and led to increased tensions in regions such as the South China Sea.

China's expanding global presence has also raised questions about its approach to human rights and governance. The Chinese government's policies regarding political dissent, censorship, and surveillance have drawn criticism from human rights organizations and some Western nations. The treatment of ethnic minority groups, such as the Uighurs in Xinjiang, has also been a subject of international concern.

China's economic and technological advancements have given it the capability to shape global norms and standards. The country's development of cutting-edge technologies like artificial intelligence and 5G has positioned it as a potential leader in the digital age. However, debates about data privacy, cybersecurity, and the potential risks associated with China's technological dominance continue to surface.

China's trajectory from the Maoist era to its current position as a global power has been a complex and multifaceted journey. The country has experienced remarkable economic growth and development, lifting millions of people out of poverty and achieving significant advancements in various sectors. However, this transformation has also come with challenges, including environmental degradation, social inequality, and concerns about human rights and political freedoms.

As China continues to exert its influence on the global stage, the international community will need to navigate the complexities of engaging with a rising power that possesses a unique political system, distinct cultural values, and a different vision for its role in the world. Balancing economic cooperation with issues of global governance, human rights, and regional stability will be crucial in shaping the future dynamics between China and the rest of the world.

In conclusion, the Maoist era and China's period of isolationism marked a significant chapter in the country's history, shaping its political, economic, and social landscape. The subsequent opening up of China brought about dramatic changes, propelling the country to become a major global player. However, this transformation has come with both opportunities and challenges, prompting ongoing debates and discussions about China's domestic policies, international engagement, and its aspirations for global leadership. The relationship between China and the rest of the world continues to evolve, with implications that extend far beyond the nation's borders.

Deng Xiaoping and the Opening Up: A Paradigm Shift in China's Development

Deng Xiaoping, a pivotal figure in modern Chinese history, spearheaded a series of economic and political reforms that transformed China into a global economic powerhouse. His policies, collectively known as "Opening Up" or "Reform and Opening Up," ushered in an era of unprecedented growth, liberalization, and international engagement. Deng's visionary leadership and pragmatic approach revitalized China's economy, reshaped its political landscape, and reshaped the global order.

This essay aims to provide a comprehensive overview of Deng Xiaoping's role in China's opening up and examine the profound impact it had on the country's development trajectory. By analyzing the historical context, key reforms, and outcomes of Deng's policies, we will delve into the reasons behind their success and explore the challenges they presented. Furthermore, this essay will assess the broader implications of China's opening up on global economics, trade, and geopolitics.

Historical Context

To understand the significance of Deng Xiaoping's reforms, it is essential to examine the historical context that preceded them. After the establishment of the People's Republic of China in 1949 under the leadership of Mao Zedong, the country embarked on a path of socialist planned economy and isolated itself from the global stage. Mao's policies, such as the Great Leap Forward and the Cultural Revolution, brought about disastrous consequences, resulting in economic stagnation, political instability, and social upheaval.

Deng Xiaoping emerged as a leader during the post-Mao era when China was grappling with the aftermath of these policies. Deng recognized the urgent need for change and aimed to revitalize the nation by implementing market-oriented reforms and opening up to the world. His approach diverged from Mao's orthodox Marxist ideology and emphasized practicality, pragmatism, and the pursuit of economic development.

Key Reforms and Policy Shifts

Agricultural Reforms: Deng's opening up began with a focus on agriculture, recognizing it as the foundation of China's economy. In 1978, he introduced the "Household Responsibility System," which replaced collective farming with individual household contracts. This reform allowed farmers to retain a portion of their harvest after meeting state quotas, effectively incentivizing productivity and spurring rural development. As a result, agricultural output soared, providing a surplus for industrialization and improving living standards in rural areas.

Special Economic Zones (SEZs): To attract foreign investment and promote export-oriented industries, Deng established Special Economic Zones in selected coastal regions such as Shenzhen, Zhuhai, and Xiamen. These zones offered preferential policies, tax incentives, and relaxed regulations to encourage foreign businesses to set up operations. The SEZs served as experimental laboratories for market-oriented reforms, testing capitalist practices within a controlled environment and gradually expanding their influence to other parts of the country.

Industrial Reforms: Deng recognized the importance of industrialization for China's development. He introduced policies to decentralize economic decision-making, promote competition, and grant greater autonomy to state-owned enterprises (SOEs). Deng encouraged the establishment of Township and Village Enterprises (TVEs) to drive rural industrialization, fostered technological advancements, and implemented price and wage reforms. These measures revitalized China's industrial sector, enhancing efficiency, productivity, and technological innovation.

Foreign Direct Investment and Trade Liberalization: Deng Xiaoping actively sought foreign investment and promoted trade liberalization as crucial drivers of economic growth. He initiated policies to attract foreign capital, establish joint ventures, and encourage technology transfer. Furthermore, Deng played a pivotal role in China's accession to the World Trade Organization (WTO) in 2001, opening up China's markets to international trade and fostering deeper integration into the global economy.

Outcomes and Deng Xiaoping's opening up policies had far-reaching consequences that transformed China's economic, social, and political landscape.

Economic Growth and Poverty Reduction: One of the most remarkable outcomes of Deng's reforms was China's unprecedented economic growth. The country experienced rapid industrialization, urbanization, and modernization, becoming the world's second-largest economy. Deng's market-oriented policies stimulated investment, increased productivity, and expanded the manufacturing sector. China's GDP grew at an average annual rate of nearly 10% during the reform era, lifting millions of people out of poverty and improving living standards.

Foreign Direct Investment and Trade Expansion: Deng's efforts to attract foreign direct investment (FDI) and liberalize trade propelled China's integration into the global economy. The establishment of Special Economic Zones and the implementation of favorable policies encouraged multinational corporations to invest in China, fostering technology transfer, job creation, and export-oriented industries. China emerged as the "factory of the world," benefiting from a vast network of global supply chains and becoming a major player in international trade.

Modernization of Agriculture: Deng's agricultural reforms brought about significant improvements in China's rural sector. The shift from collective farming to the Household Responsibility System allowed farmers to have greater control over their land and production. Agricultural productivity surged, ensuring food security and creating surplus for industrialization. The reforms also led to the development of agribusiness, the introduction of modern farming techniques, and the rise of agricultural enterprises, contributing to rural prosperity.

Urbanization and Infrastructure Development: Deng's reforms spurred rapid urbanization as millions of people migrated from rural areas to cities in search of better economic opportunities. The government invested heavily in infrastructure development, constructing roads, railways, ports, and modernizing urban centers. This urban transformation created employment, facilitated the growth of service industries, and laid the foundation for China's emergence as a global manufacturing and technology hub.

Technological Advancements and Innovation: Deng Xiaoping recognized the importance of technological progress for China's development. His policies encouraged research and development, fostered innovation, and promoted technological collaboration with foreign partners. As a result, China made significant strides in various sectors, including telecommunications, information technology, renewable energy, and high-speed rail. The country became a global leader in areas such as e-commerce, mobile payments, and artificial intelligence.

Social Changes and Rise of the Middle Class: **Deng's** economic reforms brought about social changes, including the emergence of a growing middle class. Urbanization, economic opportunities, and improved living standards contributed to the expansion of the middle-income segment of society. The rise of the middle class brought about shifts in consumption patterns, aspirations, and demands for better governance, leading to social and political implications.

Challenges and Criticisms

Despite its remarkable achievements, Deng Xiaoping's opening up policies faced several challenges and criticisms.

Growing Income Inequality: China's rapid economic growth also resulted in a significant wealth gap. The benefits of reform were not distributed equally, leading to rising income inequality and regional disparities. Coastal regions and urban areas experienced more significant development compared to rural and inland areas, exacerbating social and economic imbalances.

Environmental Concerns: The rapid pace of industrialization and urbanization brought about severe environmental challenges. Pollution, deforestation, and resource depletion became pressing issues. Deng's focus on economic growth sometimes came at the expense of environmental sustainability. However, in later years, the Chinese government recognized the importance of environmental protection and began implementing measures to address these concerns.

Political Constraints and Human Rights: Deng's reforms primarily focused on economic liberalization while maintaining tight political control. The Chinese Communist Party retained its monopoly on power, limiting political freedoms, and suppressing dissent. The government's approach to human rights, including issues related to human rights, freedom of expression, and political dissent, has been a subject of criticism and concern both domestically and internationally.

State-Owned Enterprises and Market Distortions: Despite efforts to introduce market-oriented reforms, China's state-owned enterprises (SOEs) continue to play a significant role in the economy. The dominance of SOEs in strategic sectors has created market distortions, inefficiencies, and a lack of fair competition. Balancing the need for economic liberalization with the role of the state remains a complex challenge for China.

Geopolitical and Trade Tensions: China's economic rise and its integration into the global economy have led to geopolitical tensions and trade disputes with other countries. Concerns have been raised regarding intellectual property rights, market access, and fair trade practices. The Belt and Road Initiative, China's ambitious infrastructure and connectivity project, has also faced criticism for its potential geopolitical implications.

Implications on Global Economics and Geopolitics

Dcng Xiaoping's opening up policies had profound implications for global economics and geopolitics.

Shifting Global Economic Order: China's rapid economic growth and its integration into the global economy have altered the dynamics of the international economic order. The country's manufacturing prowess, export competitiveness, and massive consumer market have made it a crucial player in global trade. China's rise has challenged the dominance of traditional economic powers and reshaped global supply chains.

Trade and Investment Flows: China's opening up policies have facilitated increased trade and investment flows, creating new opportunities for businesses worldwide. Many countries have sought to engage with China to access its market, attract Chinese investment, and benefit from its manufacturing capabilities. China's outbound investment and involvement in infrastructure projects through initiatives like the Belt and Road Initiative have expanded its economic influence globally.

Technological Competition: China's rapid technological advancements, particularly in areas like 5G, artificial intelligence, and digital technology, have led to increased competition in the global tech arena. The country's push for innovation and its growing pool of tech companies have challenged the dominance of Western technology firms, creating a new landscape of technological competition and cooperation.

Regional Influence: China's opening up policies have also enhanced its regional influence. Through initiatives like the Asian Infrastructure Investment Bank (AIIB) and regional trade agreements such as the Regional Comprehensive Economic Partnership (RCEP), China has sought to strengthen economic ties and foster closer integration with neighboring countries, thereby expanding its geopolitical influence in the Asia-Pacific region.

Diplomatic Relations: China's economic rise and its role as a major global player have had implications for its diplomatic relations. The country's growing economic clout has allowed it to exert influence through economic diplomacy and bilateral trade agreements. However, it has also faced diplomatic challenges due to concerns over issues such as human rights, territorial disputes, and geopolitical rivalries.

Deng Xiaoping's opening up policies marked a turning point in China's history, transforming the country from an isolated and impoverished nation into an economic powerhouse with global influence. His pragmatic approach and market-oriented reforms unleashed the potential of China's economy, leading to unprecedented growth, poverty reduction, and technological advancements. However, challenges such as income inequality, environmental degradation, and political constraints remain.

China's opening up has also reshaped the global economic landscape, triggering shifts in trade patterns, investment flows, and technological competition. It has raised geopolitical tensions while providing opportunities for economic engagement and cooperation. Understanding Deng

Xiaoping's role in China's opening up is crucial for comprehending the complexities of China's development trajectory and its impact on the world stage.

Post-Deng Xiaoping Era and Global Engagement

The post-Deng Xiaoping era in China has been marked by significant changes and transformations, both domestically and in terms of China's global engagement. Deng Xiaoping, the paramount leader of the People's Republic of China from the late 1970s until his retirement in 1992, laid the foundation for China's economic reform and opening up policies, which propelled the country to unprecedented levels of growth and development. After Deng's era, China has continued to evolve and adapt to the shifting dynamics of the global order, emerging as a major player in international affairs. This essay aims to explore the post-Deng Xiaoping era in China and analyze its impact on China's global engagement.

Historical Context: Deng Xiaoping's Reforms

To understand the post-Deng Xiaoping era, it is crucial to examine the reforms initiated by Deng himself. Deng's reforms focused on economic modernization and opening up to the outside world. He introduced the policy of "Socialism with Chinese Characteristics," which emphasized market-oriented economic reforms while maintaining the political control of the Communist Party. Deng's economic policies led to the dismantling of the state-controlled planned economy and the introduction of market mechanisms, foreign investment, and entrepreneurship. These reforms brought rapid economic growth, increased living standards, and lifted millions of people out of poverty, transforming China into an economic powerhouse.

Successors and Their Influence

Following Deng Xiaoping's retirement, a succession of leaders took the helm of the Communist Party, each leaving their mark on China's trajectory. Jiang Zemin succeeded Deng in 1992, followed by Hu Jintao in 2002, and Xi Jinping in 2012. While Deng's era laid the groundwork for economic reforms, his successors have faced new challenges and opportunities in the post-Deng Xiaoping era.

Jiang Zemin's leadership focused on consolidating the economic gains achieved under Deng and nurturing a more open and market-oriented society. During his tenure, China joined the World Trade Organization (WTO) in 2001, signifying a deeper integration into the global economy. Jiang's emphasis on technological advancement and infrastructure development set the stage for China's subsequent rise as a global manufacturing hub.

Hu Jintao, who assumed leadership in 2002, pursued a policy of "Harmonious Society," aimed at addressing domestic disparities and social issues arising from rapid economic development. Hu prioritized sustainable growth, energy conservation, and environmental protection. China's global engagement during his tenure focused on maintaining stability, building diplomatic relations, and expanding economic ties with developing nations.

Xi Jinping, the current paramount leader, has brought a significant shift in China's governance and global engagement. Under Xi's leadership, China has pursued a more assertive and proactive foreign policy, aiming to establish itself as a global power. Xi introduced the concept of the "Chinese Dream," emphasizing national rejuvenation, economic development, and comprehensive national strength. His flagship initiatives, such as the Belt and Road Initiative (BRI) and the "Made in China 2025" plan, demonstrate China's ambition to reshape global trade and investment patterns.

Economic Expansion and Global Influence

One of the defining features of the post-Deng Xiaoping era has been China's remarkable economic expansion and its increasing global influence. Deng's reforms opened the floodgates for foreign direct investment (FDI) and international trade, allowing China to become the world's largest exporter and the second-largest economy. China's economic rise has been accompanied by an expanded role in international organizations, such as the United Nations and the World Bank, and an increased influence in regional and global affairs.

China's economic growth has been a driving force behind its global engagement. The country has pursued an active policy of economic diplomacy, forging strategic partnerships and participating in regional and international economic forums. China has become a major player in global trade and investment, with its companies expanding overseas and establishing a presence in various industries around the world. The country's growing consumer market has also become an attractive destination for multinational corporations seeking to tap into its vast consumer base.

Furthermore, China's economic clout has enabled it to exert influence through initiatives like the Belt and Road Initiative (BRI). The BRI, announced by President Xi Jinping in 2013, aims to enhance connectivity and promote economic cooperation between China and countries along the ancient Silk Road routes. Through infrastructure development projects, trade agreements, and financial cooperation, China seeks to strengthen its economic ties with participating nations and expand its influence in regions such as Asia, Europe, Africa, and the Middle East.

In addition to economic engagement, China has also increased its diplomatic efforts to enhance its global influence. The country has actively pursued diplomatic relations and partnerships with nations across the globe, including both developed and developing countries. China has deepened its engagement in multilateral forums and initiatives, such as the Shanghai Cooperation Organization (SCO), BRICS (Brazil, Russia, India, China, South Africa), and the Asian Infrastructure Investment Bank (AIIB), among others. Through these platforms, China aims to shape regional and global agendas, advance its interests, and project itself as a responsible global power.

Technological Advancements and Innovation
Another significant aspect of the post-Deng Xiaoping era is China's rapid advancements in technology and innovation. Deng's economic reforms laid the foundation for technological development by opening up the country to foreign investment and knowledge exchange. Over the years, China has made substantial progress in various fields, including telecommunications, artificial intelligence, renewable energy, and high-speed rail.

China's technological advancements have not only propelled its domestic development but have also had a profound impact on its global engagement. The country has become a leading player in areas such as telecommunications, with companies like Huawei and ZTE gaining global recognition. China's technological prowess has raised concerns in some quarters, particularly regarding issues such as intellectual property theft, cybersecurity, and its impact on global competition. However, China has continued to invest in research and development, fostering an environment conducive to innovation and attracting talented scientists and engineers from around the world.

Evolving Foreign Policy and Global Challenges

The post-Deng Xiaoping era has witnessed an evolving foreign policy approach by China. While Deng emphasized "keeping a low profile" and focusing on domestic development, subsequent leaders, particularly Xi Jinping, have pursued a more proactive and assertive foreign policy. China's approach is characterized by a desire to safeguard its core interests, enhance its global standing, and shape regional and international norms in alignment with its own priorities.

China's rise as a global power has also presented a range of challenges and complexities. The country faces issues such as territorial disputes in the South China Sea, tensions with neighboring countries, trade frictions with the United States, and concerns about human rights and governance. These challenges have shaped China's global engagement and influenced its diplomatic strategies, as the country seeks to balance its national interests with maintaining stability and managing international perceptions.

China's global engagement has also faced scrutiny regarding issues of transparency, reciprocity, and adherence to international norms. Questions have been raised about China's approach to global governance, human rights, intellectual property rights, and its impact on developing nations. As China continues to expand its influence, these issues are likely to remain areas of contention and require ongoing dialogue and cooperation between China and the international community.

The post-Deng Xiaoping era in China has seen the country undergo remarkable changes and transformations in its domestic policies and global engagement. Deng Xiaoping's economic reforms set China on a path of rapid economic growth and integration into the global economy.

Part II: Foundations of Chinese Multilateralism

In an increasingly interconnected and interdependent world, multilateralism has emerged as a crucial framework for addressing global challenges and advancing international cooperation. As a rising global power, China's approach to multilateralism holds significant implications for the future of global governance and international relations. Part II of this study delves into the foundations of Chinese multilateralism, exploring the historical, ideological, and strategic factors that shape China's engagement with multilateral institutions and its vision for a new world order.

China's engagement with multilateralism is deeply rooted in its historical experience and cultural legacy. The country's long history as a civilization-state has shaped its worldview and approach to global affairs. The concept of multilateralism resonates with traditional Chinese values of harmony, cooperation, and inclusiveness, as evident in the principles of "win-win cooperation" and "peaceful development" espoused by Chinese leaders. This historical perspective provides important insights into China's motivations and priorities within the multilateral system.

Ideologically, China's multilateralism is influenced by its socialist political system and the guiding principles of the Chinese Communist Party (CCP). The CCP's emphasis on sovereignty, non-interference, and state-led development shapes China's approach to multilateral institutions. The principle of non-interference in the internal affairs of other states has been a central tenet of China's foreign policy, particularly in its engagements with developing countries. This approach sets China apart from Western powers and has garnered support from many countries seeking an alternative to the liberal democratic model.

China's strategic interests also play a significant role in shaping its engagement with multilateralism. As a rapidly growing economy and a major trading nation, China relies heavily on a stable and open global economic system. Participation in multilateral institutions such as the World Trade Organization (WTO) and regional initiatives like the Belt and Road Initiative (BRI) allows China to secure its economic interests, expand its influence, and shape the rules of the game. China's engagement with multilateralism is not only driven by economic considerations but also by strategic imperatives, including its pursuit of regional stability, resource security, and the protection of its territorial claims.

At the heart of China's multilateral strategy is its vision for a new world order that is more equitable, inclusive, and reflective of its rising global status. China seeks to reshape global governance institutions to better align with its interests and the interests of other developing countries. This vision is exemplified by China's push for reforms within existing institutions, such as the International Monetary Fund (IMF) and the United Nations Security Council (UNSC), to increase the representation and voice of emerging economies.

Furthermore, China has been actively promoting the establishment of new multilateral institutions that reflect its priorities and offer alternatives to the existing Western-dominated order. The Asian Infrastructure Investment Bank (AIIB), the New Development Bank (NDB) of the BRICS countries, and the Shanghai Cooperation Organization (SCO) are examples of China's efforts to shape the global landscape and establish platforms for cooperation outside the traditional Western-led institutions.

China's approach to multilateralism also intersects with its broader geopolitical aspirations. The Belt and Road Initiative, launched in 2013, aims to enhance connectivity and economic integration across Eurasia and beyond. Through infrastructure investments, trade facilitation, and people-to-people exchanges, China seeks to build a community of shared interests and common destiny. The BRI showcases China's multilateral approach by involving multiple countries and regions, emphasizing mutual benefits, and fostering cooperation on a global scale.

However, China's multilateralism is not without challenges and criticisms. Concerns have been raised about its adherence to international norms, human rights issues, and its growing assertiveness in regional disputes. Some argue that China's engagement with multilateralism is driven by a desire to expand its influence and reshape the global order in its favor, rather than a genuine commitment to multilateral principles. There are concerns that China may use multilateral institutions to advance its own economic and political interests at the expense of smaller, less powerful nations.

Moreover, China's emphasis on sovereignty and non-interference has been viewed as a means to shield its own domestic practices from international scrutiny, particularly regarding human rights and democratic values. Critics argue that China's approach to multilateralism lacks transparency and accountability, and that its actions within multilateral institutions may undermine the promotion of universal values and norms.

China's growing economic influence and investment activities have also raised concerns about debt sustainability, environmental impact, and potential geopolitical dependencies. Critics worry that China's economic initiatives, such as the BRI, may lead to a debt trap for developing countries, allowing China to exert undue influence and control over their economies and resources.

Furthermore, China's assertiveness in territorial disputes in the South China Sea and the East China Sea has strained its relations with neighboring countries and raised questions about its commitment to peaceful resolution and adherence to international law. These tensions have put China's multilateral approach to the test, as it navigates conflicting interests and the need to maintain regional stability.

In response to these criticisms and challenges, China has sought to enhance its diplomatic engagement, improve communication, and address concerns through dialogue and cooperation. Chinese leaders have emphasized the importance of building trust, promoting mutual understanding, and fostering a peaceful and stable international environment. China has also taken steps to address issues related to debt sustainability and environmental sustainability within its multilateral initiatives.

China's growing influence within multilateral institutions has prompted other major powers, particularly the United States, to reassess their own approaches to multilateralism. The shifting dynamics of global power and China's assertive posture have sparked debates and competition over the future direction of multilateralism. Some view

China's rise as a challenge to the existing liberal international order, while others see opportunities for collaboration and the potential for a more inclusive and multipolar system.

The foundations of Chinese multilateralism are complex and multifaceted, shaped by historical, ideological, and strategic factors. China's approach to multilateralism reflects its aspirations as a rising global power, its desire to shape global governance institutions, and its pursuit of its own interests and vision for a new world order. However, China's engagement with multilateralism also faces challenges and criticisms, including concerns about its adherence to international norms, human rights issues, and its assertive behavior in regional disputes.

Understanding the foundations of Chinese multilateralism is crucial for comprehending China's role in shaping the future of global governance and international relations. As China continues to expand its influence and engage with multilateral institutions, it will be essential to monitor the evolving dynamics and implications of its multilateral approach on the global stage.

China's Participation in International Organizations: A Global Power's Expanding Role

China's rapid rise as a global power has been accompanied by its growing participation and influence in international organizations. As the world's most populous country and second-largest economy, China's engagement in these multilateral institutions has far-reaching implications for global governance, regional stability, and the advancement of its national interests. This introduction provides an overview of China's involvement in international organizations, highlighting its motivations, impact, challenges, and prospects.

Historical Context:

China's engagement with international organizations can be traced back to its initial membership in the United Nations (UN) in 1971, replacing the Republic of China (Taiwan). This event marked a turning point in China's diplomatic strategy, as it sought to shed its self-imposed isolation and adopt a more active role in global affairs. Since then, China's involvement in international organizations has expanded significantly, reflecting its growing political, economic, and military influence on the global stage.

Motivations for Participation:

China's participation in international organizations is driven by a combination of strategic, economic, and political motivations. Strategically, China seeks to shape the global order to better align with its national interests and challenge the dominance of Western powers. Economically, China aims to leverage international organizations to gain access to new markets, secure resources, and promote its ambitious Belt and Road Initiative (BRI). Politically, China uses these platforms to enhance its soft power, project influence, and enhance its international reputation.

Impact on Global Governance:

China's increased participation in international organizations has had a significant impact on global governance structures. China's growing influence in the UN, World Trade Organization (WTO), International Monetary Fund (IMF), and other organizations has led to calls for reforms to better reflect the changing global power dynamics. This shift has challenged the dominance of Western powers and fostered a more multipolar international system. However, China's rising influence has also raised concerns about its adherence to international norms, human rights, and its commitment to a rules-based order.

Regional and Global Stability:

China's participation in regional and global organizations has played a crucial role in promoting stability and addressing regional challenges. In the case of Asia, China's active involvement in the Association of Southeast Asian Nations (ASEAN), Shanghai Cooperation Organization (SCO), and other forums has helped mitigate regional tensions, enhance economic integration, and facilitate cooperation on issues such as maritime disputes and security threats. However, China's assertive actions in the South China Sea and its territorial disputes with neighboring countries have strained its relations with regional partners and raised concerns about its intentions.

Challenges and Criticisms:

China's growing participation in international organizations has not been without challenges and criticisms. Some argue that China's expanding influence comes at the expense of smaller states, as it uses its economic leverage to push for its own interests. Others raise concerns about China's human rights record, lack of transparency, and potential for undue influence in decision-making processes. Additionally, China's Belt and Road Initiative (BRI) has also faced criticism for promoting debt traps, environmental damage, and undermining the sovereignty of recipient countries. These criticisms and challenges have highlighted the need for greater transparency, accountability, and adherence to international norms by China.

Prospects for the Future:

China's participation in international organizations is likely to continue expanding in the future, reflecting its growing global influence and ambition to shape the international order. As China seeks to establish itself as a leading global power, it will increasingly use multilateral platforms to advance its interests and enhance its international standing. However, as China's influence grows, it will also face greater scrutiny and challenges from other countries and international actors. The key question remains whether China will continue to adhere to the existing international norms and rules or will seek to reshape them to reflect its own interests and values.

China's participation in international organizations has become increasingly important in shaping global governance, promoting regional and global stability, and advancing its national interests. While China's growing influence has been met with challenges and criticisms, its expanding role offers opportunities for greater cooperation, mutual benefits, and constructive engagement. The future of China's participation in international organizations will depend on its ability to balance its own interests with the needs and concerns of other countries, and its willingness to uphold the principles of transparency, accountability, and respect for international norms.

China's Role in the United Nations: Shaping Global Governance

The United Nations (UN) serves as an international platform for countries to come together, collaborate, and address global challenges. As one of the founding members, China has played a significant role in shaping the UN's agenda and policies since its inception. Over the years, China's influence within the UN has grown exponentially, reflecting its status as a global power and its evolving foreign policy objectives. This essay aims to explore China's role in the United Nations, examining its contributions, interests, and challenges within the international organization.

China's Journey in the United Nations:

China's involvement in the United Nations can be traced back to its founding in 1945. Despite its tumultuous domestic and international circumstances during that time, China was recognized as one of the five permanent members of the UN Security Council, granting it significant decision-making power within the organization.

This recognition marked China's reemergence as a major global player after years of internal conflicts and foreign interventions.

Initially, China's role in the UN was primarily focused on the country's political recognition and representation on the global stage. However, as China's influence and capabilities grew, it started actively engaging in multilateral diplomacy, contributing to various UN bodies and initiatives. China's involvement spans a wide range of areas, including peacekeeping operations, economic development, human rights, climate change, and global health.

China's Contributions to the United Nations:

Peacekeeping Operations:
China has consistently been one of the largest contributors to UN peacekeeping operations, showcasing its commitment to maintaining international peace and security. It has provided

troops, police officers, and financial support to numerous peacekeeping missions worldwide. China's peacekeeping efforts reflect its aspiration to promote a stable global order and enhance its image as a responsible international actor.

Economic Development and Sustainable Development Goals (SDGs):

China's economic rise and its emphasis on development have positioned the country as a significant player in advancing the UN's sustainable development agenda. As the world's second-largest economy, China has contributed substantial financial resources and expertise to support development projects in developing countries. Moreover, China's Belt and Road Initiative (BRI), a massive infrastructure project, has the potential to contribute significantly to achieving the SDGs by improving connectivity and fostering economic growth across regions.

Climate Change:

China's role in combating climate change has become increasingly prominent in recent years. As the largest emitter of greenhouse gases, China's commitment to addressing climate change is crucial for global efforts. China has participated actively in international climate negotiations, such as the Paris Agreement, and has taken significant steps to reduce its carbon emissions. Its investment in renewable energy technologies and promotion of green initiatives demonstrate its dedication to combating climate change and transitioning towards a more sustainable future.

Global Health:

China's engagement in global health initiatives has gained prominence, particularly in the context of the COVID-19 pandemic. China played a crucial role in providing medical assistance, sharing expertise, and supporting vaccine distribution to countries in need. It has also worked closely with the World Health Organization (WHO) to enhance global health governance and contribute to the development of international health regulations.

China's Interests and Challenges in the United Nations:

While China has made substantial contributions to the United Nations, its involvement is not without challenges and controversies. Understanding China's interests and the challenges it faces within the UN framework is essential for comprehending its role accurately.

National Sovereignty and Non-interference:
China strongly upholds the principles of national sovereignty and non-interference in the internal affairs of other states. This stance often poses challenges when addressing human rights issues or situations of internal conflict within member states. China's interpretation of these principles sometimes clashes with other member states

advocating for humanitarian intervention or the promotion of human rights.

Power

Power Dynamics and Geopolitical Competition: China's rising influence within the United Nations has led to shifts in power dynamics and geopolitical competition. As China's economic and military capabilities grow, some countries express concerns about its increasing influence over UN decision-making processes. This dynamic can create tensions and divisions within the organization, particularly when it comes to issues such as regional conflicts, sanctions, or human rights.

Human Rights Concerns: China's approach to human rights has been a subject of scrutiny and controversy. Its record on issues such as freedom of expression, religious freedom, and minority rights has drawn criticism from human rights organizations and some member states. China's permanent membership in the UN Security Council and its veto power can limit the organization's ability to address human rights violations, especially when they occur within its own borders or those of its allies.

Taiwan and the One-China Policy:

The issue of Taiwan remains a highly sensitive and complex matter within the United Nations. China considers Taiwan as an integral part of its territory and insists on the One-China policy, which limits Taiwan's participation in UN activities and organizations. This situation poses challenges for the UN in terms of inclusivity and representation, as Taiwan is not a recognized sovereign state but has made significant contributions in areas such as public health and disaster relief.

Balancing National Interests and Global Responsibilities:

China's expanding global role necessitates a delicate balance between its national interests and its responsibilities as a global player within the United Nations. While China seeks to protect its own interests, it is also expected to contribute to global governance and uphold the principles of the UN Charter. Striking this balance requires navigating complex geopolitical landscapes, competing priorities, and evolving alliances.

China's Future Role in the United Nations:

China's role in the United Nations is expected to continue evolving and expanding in the coming years. As the world's second-largest economy and a major global power, China's influence will likely continue to shape the organization's policies and decisions. Several factors will influence China's future role in the UN:

Continued Economic Growth and Development:
China's economic growth trajectory will play a significant role in its engagement with the United Nations. As its economy continues to expand, China

will have more resources and capabilities to contribute to development projects, poverty alleviation, and sustainable development initiatives. Its success in achieving its domestic development goals will also influence its standing within the international community.

Global Leadership Ambitions:

China's aspirations for global leadership will likely drive its engagement within the United Nations. As it seeks to increase its influence and shape global governance, China may pursue leadership roles in UN bodies and initiatives, advocate for its own policy preferences, and strive to establish new norms and rules in areas such as technology, trade, and climate change.

Balancing National Interests and Global Responsibilities:

China's ability to strike a balance between its national interests and its global responsibilities will determine its effectiveness and acceptance within the United Nations. As China's global footprint expands, it will face increasing expectations to contribute to global challenges and play a constructive role in addressing pressing issues such as climate change, poverty, and conflict resolution.

Multilateral Engagement and Cooperation:
China's approach to multilateralism and cooperation will shape its relationships with other member states and influence its role within the United Nations. As the world becomes more interconnected and interdependent, China's willingness to collaborate, build alliances, and find common ground with diverse stakeholders will determine its ability to shape global governance effectively.

China's role in the United Nations has significantly evolved since its founding. As a major global power, China has become an influential player within the organization, contributing to various areas such as peacekeeping operations, economic development, climate change, and global health. However, China's growing influence also raises concerns and challenges, particularly regarding human rights, power dynamics, and geopolitical competition. As China's economic and military capabilities continue to grow, its role within the United Nations is expected to expand and evolve in the coming years.

To effectively navigate these challenges and contribute to global governance, China will need to strike a balance between its national interests and its global responsibilities. It will also need to engage in multilateralism and cooperation, build alliances with diverse stakeholders, and uphold the principles of the UN Charter.

As the world faces an array of pressing issues, from climate change to regional conflicts to global health crises, the United Nations will continue to play a critical role in shaping international responses. China's engagement and role within the organization will be crucial in shaping the UN's effectiveness and influence in addressing these challenges.

China and Regional Organizations (ASEAN, SCO)

China, as the world's most populous country and one of the largest economies, holds significant influence on the global stage. Over the past few decades, China has actively engaged with regional organizations to promote its interests and expand its sphere of influence. Two notable regional organizations that China has been involved with are the Association of Southeast Asian Nations (ASEAN) and the Shanghai Cooperation Organization (SCO). ASEAN is a regional bloc consisting of ten Southeast Asian countries, while SCO is a Eurasian political, economic, and security organization comprising eight member states, including China. The relationship between China and these regional organizations has evolved over time, shaping the dynamics of regional cooperation, economic integration, and security in Asia.

This essay aims to provide an in-depth analysis of China's engagement with ASEAN and SCO, highlighting the motivations, challenges, and implications of its involvement. By examining China's approach towards these organizations, we can gain insights into its foreign policy objectives, regional strategies, and the impact on regional stability and cooperation.

Historical Context:

China's involvement with regional organizations like ASEAN and SCO can be understood in the context of its broader foreign policy goals. Following the establishment of the People's Republic of China in 1949, China initially adopted a more isolated and self-reliant approach due to ideological and geopolitical considerations. However, in the late 1970s, China embarked on a path of economic reforms and openness, which gradually led to its increased integration with the international community. As China's economic power grew, it sought to assert itself as a regional leader and enhance its regional influence.

China and ASEAN:

China's relationship with ASEAN has evolved significantly since the early 1990s when diplomatic ties were established. Initially, China's engagement with ASEAN focused primarily on economic cooperation, trade, and investment. The launch of the China-ASEAN Free Trade Area (CAFTA) in 2010 marked a significant milestone in deepening economic ties between China and ASEAN member states. China has become ASEAN's largest trading partner, while ASEAN has become China's third-largest trading partner.

Apart from economic cooperation, China has also sought to strengthen its political and strategic ties with ASEAN. In 2002, China and ASEAN signed the Declaration on the Conduct of Parties in the

South China Sea (DOC), which aimed to manage and prevent conflicts in the disputed waters. However, tensions over territorial claims in the South China Sea have strained China's relations with some ASEAN member states, particularly Vietnam and the Philippines.

China's approach to ASEAN can be characterized by its policy of "peaceful rise" or "peaceful development." China emphasizes peaceful coexistence, mutual benefit, and non-interference in the domestic affairs of other countries. China has also provided economic assistance and infrastructure development projects to ASEAN member states, contributing to its soft power in the region.

China and SCO:

China's engagement with the Shanghai Cooperation Organization (SCO) has been driven by its strategic interests in Central Asia. The SCO was founded in 2001 and originally comprised China, Russia,

Kazakhstan, Kyrgyzstan, Tajikistan, and Uzbekistan. In 2017, India and Pakistan joined as full members. The SCO serves as a platform for member states to enhance regional security cooperation, combat terrorism, and promote economic integration.

For China, the SCO is crucial for advancing its "Belt and Road Initiative" (BRI), a massive infrastructure development project aimed at enhancing connectivity and trade between Asia, Europe, and Africa. Many Central Asian countries are important partners in the BRI, providing strategic transit routes and access to energy resources. The SCO acts as a facilitator for coordination and cooperation among member states in implementing BRI projects China's engagement with the SCO is driven by several key factors. Firstly, the SCO provides a platform for China to strengthen its political and security ties with Central Asian countries. Central Asia holds strategic importance for China due to its proximity to Xinjiang, a region of China that faces security challenges, including separatism and terrorism. Through the SCO, China has been able to enhance intelligence sharing, joint military exercises, and counter-terrorism cooperation with member states, contributing to regional stability.

Secondly, the SCO offers economic benefits for China. Central Asia is rich in natural resources, including oil, gas, and minerals, which are essential for China's energy security and economic development. The SCO facilitates economic cooperation, trade, and investment between China and Central Asian countries, promoting infrastructure development, and facilitating cross-border connectivity. China has invested heavily in infrastructure projects such as roads, railways, and pipelines, which not only serve its economic interests but also strengthen its influence in the region.

Furthermore, China's involvement in the SCO aligns with its broader geopolitical objectives. As the United States has been reducing its military presence in Afghanistan, China sees an opportunity to increase its engagement in the region. The SCO provides a platform for China to work closely with Russia and Central Asian countries in addressing security challenges in Afghanistan and promoting stability in the region. China's participation in the SCO allows it to shape regional security dynamics and expand its influence beyond its immediate neighborhood.

Motivations and Challenges:

China's engagement with ASEAN and the SCO is driven by a combination of economic, political, and strategic motivations. Economically, China benefits from enhanced trade, investment, and access to resources through its engagement with these regional organizations. Politically, China seeks to strengthen its diplomatic ties, build relationships, and promote its soft power in the region. Strategically, China aims to shape regional dynamics, enhance security cooperation, and expand its influence in neighboring regions.

However, China's engagement with ASEAN and the SCO is not without challenges. In the case of ASEAN, China faces territorial disputes in the South China Sea, where its expansive claims overlap with those of several ASEAN member states. This has led to tensions, mistrust, and occasional confrontations, challenging China's efforts to build a harmonious and cooperative relationship with ASEAN as a whole. Managing these disputes and addressing the concerns of smaller ASEAN member states are ongoing challenges for China.

Similarly, China's involvement in the SCO presents challenges related to balancing the interests of different member states. The SCO comprises diverse countries with varying political systems, economic priorities, and security concerns. China must navigate these differences and work towards consensus on key issues such as counter-terrorism, regional stability, and economic integration. Additionally, China's dominant role within the SCO raises concerns among some member states about potential asymmetry in influence and decision-making processes.

Moreover, China's rise as a regional power has also attracted attention and scrutiny from external actors, particularly the United States. The increasing influence of China in ASEAN and the SCO has raised concerns about China's intentions, its adherence to international norms, and its impact on regional dynamics. The United States has sought to counterbalance China's influence by enhancing its engagement with ASEAN and strengthening alliances and partnerships in the region.

Implications and Future Outlook:

China's engagement with ASEAN and the SCO has significant implications for regional cooperation, economic integration, and security in Asia. China's economic integration with ASEAN has created both opportunities and challenges for the member states. While China has emerged as a crucial trading partner and a source of investment and infrastructure development, there are concerns about unequal economic relations, competition with local industries, and environmental impacts.

In the case of the SCO, China's involvement has contributed to the organization's growing influence and relevance in Eurasia. The SCO provides a platform for China to strengthen its political and security ties with Central Asian countries, expand its economic interests, and shape regional dynamics. However, the SCO faces challenges in balancing the interests of its diverse member states and addressing regional security issues effectively.

The future outlook of China's engagement with ASEAN and the SCO will be shaped by various factors. Firstly, the resolution of territorial disputes in the South China Sea will be crucial in determining the trajectory of China-ASEAN relations. Constructive dialogue, confidence-building measures, and adherence to international law will be essential in maintaining regional stability and fostering cooperation.

Secondly, China's role within the SCO will continue to evolve as the organization expands its scope of cooperation. The SCO's focus on counter-terrorism, regional security, and economic integration will be key areas where China's leadership and influence will be tested. As the BRI progresses, the implementation of infrastructure projects and the management of associated economic and political risks will be significant factors in China's engagement with the SCO.

Additionally, the external dynamics and the response of other major powers, particularly the United States, will have an impact on China's engagement with ASEAN and the SCO. The competition for influence in the region between

China and the United States, as well as other regional powers, may shape the future landscape of regional organizations. The extent to which China can effectively address concerns, build trust, and promote cooperation will determine its ability to consolidate its influence and shape regional dynamics.

In conclusion, China's engagement with regional organizations such as ASEAN and the SCO reflects its aspirations as a regional power. China's involvement is driven by economic, political, and strategic motivations, and it seeks to promote economic integration, strengthen political ties, and enhance its influence in neighboring regions. However, challenges such as territorial disputes, balancing diverse interests, and external scrutiny pose significant hurdles. The implications of China's engagement with ASEAN and the SCO extend beyond bilateral relationships, influencing regional stability, economic cooperation, and the balance of power in Asia. The future outlook will depend on the resolution of key issues, effective management of challenges, and the dynamics of competition and cooperation among major regional players.

China's Membership in Economic Institutions (WTO, AIIB)

China's rapid economic growth and global influence have propelled it to the forefront of the international stage. As the world's most populous nation and the second-largest economy, China has actively sought to expand its participation in global economic institutions. Two notable examples of China's engagement are its membership in the World Trade Organization (WTO) and its founding role in the Asian Infrastructure Investment Bank (AIIB). These institutions play crucial roles in shaping the global economic landscape and have significant implications for China's domestic development and its role as a global power.

In this introduction, we will explore the historical context, motivations, and implications of China's membership in these economic institutions. We will analyze the challenges and opportunities China faces as it navigates the complex dynamics of global economic governance. Furthermore, we will assess the impact of China's participation on the institutions themselves, as well as on the international order. By examining these aspects, we aim to gain a comprehensive understanding of the multifaceted nature of China's engagement in the WTO and AIIB.

Historical Context:

China's integration into the global economy has been a gradual and transformative process. Following the economic reforms initiated by Deng Xiaoping in the late 1970s, China shifted from a centrally planned economy to a market-oriented system. This transformation, coupled with its vast population and abundant resources, propelled China's economic rise and attracted global attention. As China sought to deepen its economic ties with the world, it recognized the importance of joining international economic institutions to secure its interests and influence their decision-making processes.

The World Trade Organization (WTO):

The WTO, established in 1995, serves as the primary global forum for trade negotiations, dispute settlement, and the development of international trade rules. China's accession to the WTO in 2001 marked a significant milestone in its integration into the global trading system. We will explore the motivations behind China's accession, including its desire for increased market access, improved investment opportunities, and enhanced credibility on the world stage. Additionally, we will discuss the challenges China faced during the negotiation process and the subsequent impact of its membership on its economy and global trade dynamics.

The Asian Infrastructure Investment Bank (AIIB):

The AIIB, established in 2015, represents a Chinese-led initiative aimed at addressing infrastructure gaps in the Asia-Pacific region. With a focus on funding large-scale infrastructure projects, the AIIB presents an alternative to established institutions like the World Bank and the Asian Development Bank. We will examine China's motivations for spearheading the creation of the AIIB, including its desire to exert greater influence in the region and reshape the global financial order. Furthermore, we will discuss the reactions and concerns raised by other major powers and the potential implications of the AIIB's emergence.

Implications of China's Membership:

China's membership in these economic institutions has far-reaching implications for its domestic and global aspirations. On the domestic front, joining the WTO and participating in the AIIB have facilitated economic liberalization, the deepening of market reforms, and the improvement of China's business environment. However, they have also presented challenges such as addressing disparities within China's economy, protecting domestic industries, and managing the social consequences of rapid economic transformation. Moreover, China's active engagement in these institutions has allowed it to shape the rules and norms of global economic governance, contributing to its rise as a global power.

Impact on the Institutions:

China's membership in the WTO and its founding role in the AIIB have inevitably influenced the functioning and dynamics of these institutions. In the case of the WTO, China's size, economic clout, and increasing assertiveness have raised questions about the institution's ability to adapt and accommodate its evolving role. We will examine China's impact on the WTO's decision-making processes, dispute settlement mechanisms, and the negotiation of new trade agreements. Regarding the AIIB, China's leading position has prompted discussions about its governance structure, lending practices, and potential competition with existing institutions. We will analyze the AIIB's role in infrastructure financing and its implications for regional and global development initiatives.

China's Role in Global Economic Governance:
China's membership in the WTO and its establishment of the AIIB reflect its broader aspirations for a greater say in global economic governance. We will discuss China's efforts to reform existing institutions, advocate for its interests, and promote alternative approaches to global economic issues. This includes initiatives such as the Belt and Road Initiative (BRI), which seeks to enhance connectivity and trade along key transport corridors. We will explore the implications of China's expanding influence on the existing global economic order and the responses from other major powers.

Challenges and Controversies:

China's membership in these economic institutions has not been without challenges and controversies. Concerns have been raised regarding China's compliance with WTO rules, including issues related to intellectual property rights, market access barriers, and state subsidies. Similarly, the AIIB has faced scrutiny over governance standards, environmental and social safeguards, and potential debt sustainability risks. We will analyze these challenges and controversies and their impact on China's reputation, as well as on the legitimacy and effectiveness of the institutions themselves.

Future Prospects and Conclusion:

Looking ahead, China's membership in the WTO and its involvement in the AIIB will continue to shape global economic governance and influence the trajectory of China's domestic development. As China seeks to address its own economic challenges, such as transitioning to a more sustainable and innovation-driven economy, its role in these institutions will evolve. We will explore the potential opportunities and risks associated with China's future engagement, including the need for continued reforms, addressing international concerns, and navigating geopolitical tensions.

In conclusion, China's membership in the WTO and its founding role in the AIIB exemplify its ambition to become a major player in global economic governance. Its engagement in these institutions has allowed China to secure its economic interests, shape global trade rules, and assert its influence on the international stage. However, it has also presented challenges and controversies that require careful management. Understanding the motivations, implications, and dynamics of China's membership in these economic institutions is crucial for comprehending the evolving landscape of global economic governance and China's role within it.

China's Approach to Multilateral Diplomacy

In today's interconnected and interdependent world, multilateral diplomacy plays a crucial role in addressing global challenges and fostering international cooperation. As one of the world's major powers, China's approach to multilateral diplomacy holds significant implications for the global order, regional stability, and the pursuit of common goals. Over the years, China has emerged as an influential player, actively participating in various multilateral institutions and shaping the discourse on international affairs. Understanding China's approach to multilateral diplomacy is essential for comprehending its evolving role in global governance and its impact on the international system.

This essay aims to provide a comprehensive introduction to China's approach to multilateral diplomacy. It will explore the key principles that underpin China's multilateral engagement, examine the country's participation in major multilateral organizations, analyze its bilateral and regional diplomatic initiatives, and assess its challenges and opportunities in the realm of multilateralism.

Historical Context:

To understand China's current approach to multilateral diplomacy, it is important to consider its historical context. China's diplomatic philosophy has evolved significantly since the founding of the People's Republic of China in 1949. During the early years of the Cold War, China adopted a revolutionary stance and focused on ideological diplomacy. However, following Deng Xiaoping's reforms in the late 1970s, China embarked on a path of economic development and integration into the international system. This shift laid the foundation for China's active engagement in multilateral diplomacy in subsequent decades.

Key Principles of China's Multilateral Engagement:

China's approach to multilateral diplomacy is guided by a set of core principles that reflect its national interests, historical experiences, and strategic objectives. These principles include:

2.1. Sovereignty and Non-Interference:

China strongly upholds the principle of sovereignty and non-interference in the internal affairs of other states. It argues that each country should have the right to determine its own political, economic, and social systems without external interference. This principle is particularly emphasized when addressing sensitive issues such as human rights and territorial disputes.

2.2. Peaceful Coexistence and Harmony:

China places great importance on maintaining peace and promoting harmonious relations among nations. It advocates for peaceful coexistence, respect for diversity, and the peaceful resolution of conflicts through dialogue and negotiation. The concept of "win-win" cooperation is central to China's diplomatic discourse, emphasizing mutual benefits and shared development.

2.3. Mutual Respect and Equality:

China emphasizes the principle of mutual respect and equality in its multilateral engagements. It insists on equal participation and treatment of all countries, regardless of their size or level of development. China often portrays itself as a defender of the interests of developing countries and a champion of a more equitable international order.

China's Participation in Major Multilateral Organizations:

China's participation in multilateral organizations has increased significantly in recent decades. It has become an active member of various international institutions, exerting influence and shaping global governance. Some of the key organizations in which China participates include:

3.1. United Nations (UN):

As a permanent member of the UN Security Council, China has a significant role in shaping global security and peacekeeping operations. China supports the UN's central role in addressing global challenges, promoting development, and safeguarding international norms and principles.

3.2. World Trade Organization (WTO):

China's accession to the WTO in 2001 marked a milestone in its integration into the global economy. As the world's largest trading nation, China plays a crucial role in international trade negotiations and advocates for a more inclusive and balanced global trade system.

3.3. Asian Infrastructure Investment Bank (AIIB):

The AIIB, initiated by China in 2015, aims to promote infrastructure development in Asia. China aspires to position the AIIB as a complementary institution to existing multilateral development banks, providing alternative financing options and promoting regional connectivity.

3.4. Shanghai Cooperation Organization (SCO):

China is a founding member of the SCO, an intergovernmental organization focused on security, economic cooperation, and cultural exchanges in Eurasia. Through the SCO, China seeks to enhance regional stability, counterterrorism efforts, and promote economic integration among member states.

China's approach to multilateral diplomacy is not confined to global organizations. It also engages in bilateral and regional diplomatic initiatives, which serve as important mechanisms to promote its interests and expand its influence. Notable initiatives include:

4.1. Belt and Road Initiative (BRI):

Launched in 2013, the BRI is China's ambitious infrastructure and economic development project that aims to enhance connectivity and cooperation across Asia, Europe, Africa, and beyond. Through the BRI, China seeks to promote economic integration, trade facilitation, and people-to-people exchanges, while also advancing its geopolitical interests.

4.2. China-ASEAN Cooperation:

China maintains a strategic partnership with the Association of Southeast Asian Nations (ASEAN). It actively engages with ASEAN through various mechanisms, such as the China-ASEAN Free Trade Area and the ASEAN Regional Forum. China's engagement with ASEAN reflects its desire to maintain regional stability, enhance economic cooperation, and mitigate potential sources of conflict in the South China Sea.

4.3. Forum on China-Africa Cooperation (FOCAC):

China has established a comprehensive partnership with African countries through the FOCAC. The forum serves as a platform for political dialogue, economic cooperation, and development assistance. China's engagement with Africa is motivated by its quest for natural resources, expanding markets, and strategic influence.

Challenges and Opportunities:

China's approach to multilateral diplomacy is not without challenges and controversies. Some concerns and criticisms include:

5.1. Human Rights and Democracy:

China's emphasis on non-interference and its track record on human rights have drawn criticism from Western countries and human rights organizations. China's approach to multilateralism often prioritizes stability and economic development over human rights and democratic values, leading to tensions in multilateral forums.

5.2. Power Competition and Geopolitics:

China's rise as a global power has generated anxieties among some countries, particularly the United States and its allies. The perception of China's assertiveness and its expanding influence in multilateral institutions has raised concerns about power competition and potential disruptions to the existing global order.

5.3. Transparency and Governance:

China's engagement in multilateral institutions has raised questions about transparency and governance. Critics argue that China's decision-making processes are often opaque, and its state-led economic model may result in asymmetrical power dynamics and unequal benefits within multilateral frameworks.

Despite these challenges, China's approach to multilateral diplomacy also presents opportunities for collaboration and positive outcomes:

5.4. Global Challenges:

China's active engagement in multilateralism provides an opportunity for addressing pressing global challenges, such as climate change, nuclear non-proliferation, and public health crises. China's commitment to the Paris Agreement and its role in the United Nations Framework Convention on

Climate Change (UNFCCC) demonstrates its willingness to collaborate on these critical issues.

5.5. Economic Cooperation:

China's economic strength and its focus on connectivity initiatives, such as the BRI, present opportunities for infrastructure development, trade facilitation, and economic cooperation. These initiatives have the potential to contribute to regional and global economic growth and development.

5.6. Multilateral Reform:

China's rising influence in multilateral institutions has prompted discussions about the need for reform and greater representation. China's active participation can serve as a catalyst for adapting and improving multilateral institutions to better reflect the evolving global landscape and address the interests and concerns of a more diverse set of actors.

China's approach to multilateral diplomacy is shaped by its national interests, historical context, and core principles. It actively participates in major multilateral organizations, engages in bilateral and regional diplomatic initiatives, and promotes its vision of a more equitable and inclusive international order. While facing challenges and criticisms, China's multilateral engagement also presents opportunities for collaboration and positive outcomes.

Understanding China's approach to multilateral diplomacy is crucial for comprehending its role in global governance, its impact on the international system, and the dynamics of power and cooperation in the 21st century. As China continues to rise as a global power, its approach to multilateralism will significantly influence the trajectory of global affairs and shape the future of multilateral cooperation.

Principles Guiding China's Multilateral Engagement

China's rise as a global power has been accompanied by an increasing emphasis on multilateralism and active participation in international organizations. Over the past few decades, China has adopted a set of principles that guide its multilateral engagement. These principles reflect China's evolving role in the international arena and its commitment to shaping global governance structures. Understanding these guiding principles is essential to comprehending China's approach to multilateralism and its aspirations in international relations.

This essay aims to explore the principles that underpin China's multilateral engagement and shed light on the country's motivations and strategies. By analyzing China's behavior within multilateral frameworks, such as the United Nations (UN), the World Trade Organization (WTO), and regional organizations like the Shanghai Cooperation Organization (SCO), we can gain insights into

China's objectives and its evolving role in shaping global norms and institutions.

A fundamental principle guiding China's multilateral engagement is its unwavering commitment to respect the sovereignty and territorial integrity of nations. China staunchly adheres to the principle of non-interference in the internal affairs of other countries, which it considers a cornerstone of international relations. This principle is rooted in China's historical experiences, where it faced interference from external powers, and it reflects China's emphasis on mutual respect and equality among nations.

China's non-interference principle often manifests in its diplomatic approach, where it refrains from intervening in the domestic affairs of other states. This approach is particularly evident in China's foreign policy stance towards issues such as human rights and democracy, where it emphasizes the importance of domestic solutions and rejects the imposition of external values or models.

Win-Win Cooperation and Shared Development: China places a strong emphasis on win-win cooperation and shared development as guiding principles in its multilateral engagement. This approach aligns with China's pursuit of its own development goals while promoting broader global prosperity. Through initiatives like the Belt and Road Initiative (BRI) and the Asian Infrastructure Investment Bank (AIIB), China seeks to foster economic connectivity, infrastructure development, and trade cooperation across regions.

China's focus on win-win cooperation emphasizes the importance of mutual benefits, balanced outcomes, and common development. It often engages in economic partnerships that leverage its resources, capital, and market to support infrastructure projects and promote economic growth in developing countries. This approach helps China build alliances, expand its influence, and ensure its economic interests are served in an interconnected global system.

China's commitment to peaceful development is another key principle guiding its multilateral engagement. The country has consistently emphasized the peaceful resolution of disputes, the promotion of stability, and the avoidance of military confrontation. China's peaceful development principle stems from its historical experiences of colonialism and conflict, and its desire to prioritize economic growth and social stability.

China's commitment to peaceful development is often reflected in its foreign policy behavior, where it seeks to resolve territorial disputes through diplomatic negotiations and dialogue. It emphasizes the importance of maintaining regional stability and advocates for the peaceful settlement of conflicts, particularly in regions like the South China Sea and the Korean Peninsula. By prioritizing peaceful development, China aims to enhance its global standing and project itself as a responsible global power.

Multilateralism and Global Governance:
China's engagement in multilateral institutions and its support for global governance mechanisms represent another principle that guides its multilateral approach. China recognizes the importance of multilateralism in addressing global challenges and believes that international cooperation is essential for maintaining peace, stability, and sustainable development.

China actively participates in multilateral organizations, such as the UN, WTO, and regional forums, to shape global norms and institutions. It seeks to influence decision-making processes and promote its interests while advocating for a more equitable and inclusive international order. China's engagement in these organizations allows it to contribute to the formulation of global rules, standards, and norms, ensuring that they reflect the interests and perspectives of developing countries.

China's support for multilateralism also extends to its active involvement in initiatives like the Paris Agreement on climate change and the Joint Comprehensive Plan of Action (JCPOA) on Iran's nuclear program. By participating in these multilateral efforts, China aims to address global challenges, demonstrate its commitment to collective action, and enhance its international reputation as a responsible stakeholder.

Respect for Diversity and Cultural Pluralism:
China places great importance on respecting diversity and cultural pluralism in its multilateral engagement. As a country with a rich cultural heritage and a diverse population, China recognizes the value of cultural diversity and the need to

protect and promote different civilizations and traditions.

China advocates for an inclusive and tolerant approach that respects the cultural rights of all nations. It opposes cultural hegemony and supports the preservation of cultural diversity within the framework of international cooperation. This principle is reflected in China's promotion of cultural exchanges, educational programs, and people-to-people exchanges, which aim to foster mutual understanding, respect, and appreciation among different cultures.

Gradual Reform and Institutional Innovation:
China acknowledges the need for reform and institutional innovation within multilateral frameworks to address the evolving global landscape. While advocating for the preservation of existing institutions, China also recognizes the importance of adapting and improving them to

better reflect the changing dynamics of the international order.

China has called for reforming global governance structures to make them more representative, inclusive, and responsive to the needs of developing countries. It seeks to enhance the voice and participation of emerging economies and developing nations in decision-making processes, particularly in institutions like the UN Security Council and the IMF. China's push for reform is driven by its aspiration to create a fairer and more balanced global order that better accommodates the interests and concerns of all nations.

China's multilateral engagement is guided by a set of principles that reflect its evolving role as a global power. The principles of respect for sovereignty and non-interference, win-win cooperation and shared development, commitment to peaceful development, multilateralism and global governance, respect for diversity and cultural pluralism, and gradual reform and institutional innovation shape China's approach to international relations and its participation in multilateral organizations.

Understanding these principles is crucial for comprehending China's motivations, strategies, and aspirations in the realm of global governance. As China continues to assert its influence and shape the international order, it remains committed to actively engaging in multilateral frameworks, promoting its interests, and contributing to the development of global rules and norms.

While China's principles may sometimes differ from those of Western powers, they reflect its unique historical experiences, domestic priorities, and vision for a more equitable and inclusive world. By examining these guiding principles, we can gain valuable insights into China's approach to multilateralism and its contributions to the evolving global order.

Multilateralism with Chinese Characteristics: Navigating a New Global Order

In recent years, the international system has witnessed a significant shift in power dynamics and the emergence of new global players. Among these players, China stands out as a rising power, asserting its influence on various fronts, including the economic, political, and diplomatic arenas. As China's global presence continues to expand, it is increasingly seeking to shape the global order in a manner that aligns with its own interests and values. This has led to the concept of "Multilateralism with Chinese Characteristics" gaining prominence in discussions surrounding global governance. In this introduction, we will explore the key aspects and implications of this concept, shedding light on China's approach to multilateralism and its potential impact on the evolving international system.

Multilateralism refers to the practice of coordinating policies and actions among multiple states to address common challenges and achieve shared goals. It is based on the principles of inclusivity, cooperation, and respect for sovereignty. Historically, multilateralism has been closely associated with Western-led institutions such as the United Nations (UN), the World Trade Organization (WTO), and the International Monetary Fund (IMF). These institutions have played a vital role in fostering collaboration among nations and facilitating global governance.

The Rise of China and Its Impact on Multilateralism

The rapid rise of China as an economic powerhouse and a global player has had profound implications for the existing multilateral order. As China's economic influence grows, it seeks to translate its economic clout into increased political and diplomatic leverage. This has led to the creation of alternative institutions, such as the Asian Infrastructure Investment Bank (AIIB) and the Belt and Road Initiative (BRI), which challenge the established Western-led order and reflect China's aspirations for a more prominent role in global governance.

Key Features of Multilateralism with Chinese Characteristics

Multilateralism with Chinese Characteristics represents China's vision for a reimagined global order that reflects its own political, economic, and cultural values. Some of the key features of this concept include:

a) Sovereignty and Non-interference: China places a strong emphasis on the principles of sovereignty and non-interference in its approach to multilateralism. It advocates for respect for national sovereignty and opposes external intervention in the internal affairs of other nations. This stance is particularly relevant to China's relationship with authoritarian regimes, which it often supports on the grounds of non-interference.

b) Economic Integration: China's economic prowess and its focus on economic development are central to its approach to multilateralism. The BRI, for example, aims to enhance connectivity and trade across Asia, Europe, and Africa through infrastructure development. By promoting economic integration, China seeks to expand its influence and create new markets for its goods and services.

c) Cooperative Security: China emphasizes the importance of cooperative security arrangements based on dialogue and mutual trust. It advocates for a regional and global security architecture that is inclusive, non-confrontational, and built on consensus. This approach is evident in China's engagement with regional organizations like the

Shanghai Cooperation Organization (SCO) and the Association of Southeast Asian Nations (ASEAN).

d) Development Assistance: China's engagement in multilateralism is also characterized by its approach to development assistance. Through initiatives like the AIIB and the Forum on China-Africa Cooperation (FOCAC), China provides financial support and infrastructure investment to developing countries. This enables China to enhance its soft power and expand its influence in regions critical to its economic and strategic interests.

Implications and Challenges

Multilateralism with Chinese Characteristics has significant implications for the international system and global governance. However, it also presents certain challenges and concerns that need to be addressed. Some of the key implications and challenges include:

a) Power Shift and Normative Competition: China's growing influence and the concept of Multilateralism with Chinese Characteristics challenge the dominance of Western-led institutions and norms. This shift in power dynamics raises questions about the future of global governance and the potential clash of different normative frameworks. As China asserts its own values and principles, there is a need for dialogue and negotiation to find common ground and ensure the inclusivity and effectiveness of multilateralism.

b) Transparency and Accountability: China's approach to multilateralism has been criticized for its lack of transparency and accountability. Critics argue that China's investment projects, particularly under the BRI, lack transparency in terms of financial arrangements, environmental impact, and social sustainability. This raises concerns about debt sustainability, corruption, and the potential for unequal power dynamics between China and recipient countries. Enhancing transparency and accountability in China's multilateral initiatives is crucial for building trust and ensuring the long-term sustainability of these projects.

c) Human Rights and Democratic Values: China's emphasis on non-interference and sovereignty has implications for human rights and democratic values within the multilateral framework. China's support for authoritarian regimes and its record on human rights have raised concerns among Western democracies and human rights advocates. Balancing the principles of sovereignty and non-interference with the promotion of human rights and democratic values is a complex challenge that needs to be addressed for a truly inclusive and effective multilateralism.

d) Regional Fragmentation and Competition: As China expands its influence and creates alternative institutions, there is a risk of regional fragmentation and competition. The establishment of parallel institutions to existing ones, such as the AIIB, can lead to a fragmented multilateral system, with countries being forced to choose between different frameworks. This fragmentation may undermine the coherence and effectiveness of global governance and require efforts to bridge gaps and promote cooperation among different multilateral initiatives.

e) Cooperation and Conflict Resolution: Multilateralism with Chinese Characteristics provides opportunities for cooperation and conflict resolution, but it also presents challenges. China's territorial disputes in the South China Sea and its assertive actions have strained its relationships with neighboring countries and raised concerns about its commitment to peaceful resolution. Balancing China's pursuit of its interests with the need for peaceful conflict resolution and cooperation is essential for fostering stability and trust in the multilateral system.

Multilateralism with Chinese Characteristics represents China's vision for reshaping the global order to reflect its own interests, values, and aspirations. As a rising power, China seeks to assert its influence on the international stage through economic integration, cooperative security, and development assistance. While this concept offers potential benefits, it also presents challenges and concerns related to power dynamics, transparency, human rights, regional fragmentation, and conflict resolution.

Navigating the evolving global order requires open dialogue, negotiation, and cooperation among nations with diverse interests and values. It is essential to find common ground and strike a balance between China's approach to multilateralism and existing norms and principles. Emphasizing inclusivity, transparency, accountability, and the promotion of human rights and democratic values will be crucial for a sustainable and effective multilateral system that addresses global challenges and fosters global cooperation.

The Belt and Road Initiative (BRI) and Multilateral Cooperation: A Pathway to Connectivity and Development

The Belt and Road Initiative (BRI) is one of the most ambitious and expansive infrastructure projects in modern history. Announced by Chinese President Xi Jinping in 2013, the BRI aims to enhance connectivity and promote economic cooperation among countries in Asia, Europe, Africa, and beyond. This initiative has sparked significant interest and debate, as it seeks to reshape regional and global dynamics through large-scale infrastructure development, trade facilitation, and people-to-people exchanges. In this essay, we will delve into the various dimensions of the BRI and its implications for multilateral cooperation, exploring the potential benefits and challenges associated with this transformative initiative.

Understanding the Belt and Road Initiative

a) Overview: The BRI comprises two main components, namely the Silk Road Economic Belt and the 21st Century Maritime Silk Road. The Silk Road Economic Belt focuses on enhancing connectivity and promoting economic cooperation through infrastructure projects spanning land routes across Asia and Europe. The 21st Century Maritime Silk Road aims to strengthen maritime trade routes and foster cooperation among countries in Southeast Asia, Africa, and the Middle East.

b) Objectives: The BRI seeks to achieve several broad objectives, including promoting economic development, facilitating trade and investment, enhancing connectivity, fostering cultural exchanges, and strengthening regional cooperation.

The initiative aims to create a network of infrastructure projects, including roads, railways, ports, and energy pipelines, to enhance connectivity and promote economic integration.

c) Scope: The BRI encompasses a vast geographical area, with over 140 countries and international organizations showing interest in participating. This makes it a truly global initiative with wide-ranging implications for regional and global economic dynamics.

Multilateral Cooperation and the Belt and Road Initiative

a) Multilateralism and the BRI: The BRI represents an approach to multilateral cooperation that seeks to promote connectivity and development through inclusive and mutually beneficial partnerships. It encourages countries to work together on infrastructure projects, trade facilitation, and policy coordination, emphasizing the importance of multilateral institutions and frameworks.

b) Enhancing Regional Cooperation: The BRI serves as a catalyst for enhancing regional cooperation, particularly in regions such as Central Asia, South Asia, Southeast Asia, and Eastern Europe. By connecting regions through infrastructure projects, trade corridors, and economic cooperation, the BRI aims to foster greater regional integration, stimulate economic growth, and address development gaps.

c) Strengthening Global Connectivity: The BRI's emphasis on connectivity extends beyond regional cooperation, aiming to create a more interconnected world. By promoting infrastructure development and connectivity projects, the BRI seeks to bridge gaps in physical infrastructure, digital connectivity, and people-to-people exchanges, facilitating global trade, investment, and cultural understanding.

Potential Benefits of the Belt and Road Initiative for Multilateral Cooperation

a) Economic Development: The BRI has the potential to stimulate economic growth and development by providing countries with enhanced access to markets, investment opportunities, and infrastructure. Through the development of transport networks, energy projects, and industrial zones, the BRI can help unlock the economic potential of participating countries, particularly those in developing regions.

b) Trade Facilitation: The BRI aims to promote trade facilitation by reducing barriers, improving logistics, and enhancing customs procedures. By streamlining trade processes and improving connectivity, the initiative can boost cross-border trade, reduce costs, and increase market access for participating countries.

c) Infrastructure Investment: The BRI's focus on infrastructure development presents significant opportunities for investment and job creation. Participating countries can benefit from foreign direct investment (FDI) in infrastructure projects, leading to the creation of employment opportunities, technology transfers, and capacity-building.

d) Cultural Exchanges and People-to-People Exchanges: The BRI places significant importance on cultural exchanges and people-to-people connectivity. Through initiatives such as student exchanges, tourism promotion, and cultural events, the BRI aims to foster mutual understanding, cultural appreciation, and interpersonal connections among participating countries. This can contribute to stronger diplomatic ties and a more harmonious global community.

e) Energy Security: The BRI's focus on energy infrastructure, including pipelines and power projects, can contribute to enhanced energy security for participating countries. By diversifying energy sources and creating interconnectivity, the BRI helps reduce dependence on a single energy supplier, ensuring a more stable and resilient energy supply chain.

Challenges and Considerations for Multilateral Cooperation within the BRI

a) Financial Sustainability: The scale and scope of the BRI raise concerns about the financial sustainability of the projects. Some countries, particularly those with limited financial resources, may face challenges in managing the debt incurred through infrastructure investments. Ensuring responsible lending practices, transparency in project financing, and debt sustainability assessments are crucial to mitigate the risks associated with the BRI.

b) : The BRI's vast reach and involvement in sensitive regions have geopolitical implications. It has the potential to influence regional dynamics, raise concerns about the expansion of Chinese influence, and lead to competition among major powers. Balancing competing interests and ensuring that the BRI aligns with the principles of inclusivity, transparency, and respect for sovereignty are essential for maintaining regional stability and avoiding geopolitical tensions.

c) Environmental Considerations: The BRI's infrastructure projects, particularly those related to energy and transportation, may have environmental impacts. The construction of dams, railways, and ports can lead to habitat destruction, deforestation, and increased carbon emissions. Integrating environmental considerations, promoting sustainable practices, and adhering to international environmental standards are crucial for minimizing negative ecological consequences and ensuring long-term sustainability.

d) Social and Labor Rights: Large-scale infrastructure projects within the BRI can have significant social and labor implications. Issues such as land acquisition, displacement of local communities, and labor rights need to be addressed to ensure that the projects promote social well-being, respect human rights, and provide fair and safe working conditions for local communities and migrant workers involved in the construction process.

e) Governance and Transparency: The BRI's success depends on effective governance structures, transparency, and accountability. Transparency in project selection, procurement processes, and financial management is essential to build trust among participating countries and ensure that the benefits of the BRI are equitably distributed. Strengthening governance mechanisms, anticorruption measures, and adhering to international standards and best practices can help address these concerns.

The Belt and Road Initiative represents a significant endeavor to promote connectivity, economic cooperation, and development on a global scale. As a multilateral initiative, the BRI has the potential to foster regional integration, enhance trade facilitation, and promote cultural exchanges among participating countries. The initiative offers opportunities for economic growth, infrastructure investment, and job creation. However, challenges such as financial sustainability, geopolitical concerns, environmental considerations, social and labor rights, and governance and transparency need to be effectively addressed for the BRI to achieve its objectives and contribute to sustainable multilateral cooperation.

Balancing the interests and aspirations of participating countries, adhering to international norms and standards, and engaging in open dialogue and collaboration are crucial for ensuring that the BRI becomes a pathway to connectivity and development that benefits all stakeholders involved. By embracing the principles of inclusivity, transparency, and sustainability, the BRI can contribute to a more interconnected, prosperous, and cooperative world.

Part III: Key Areas of Chinese Multilateral Engagement

China's rise as a global power has been accompanied by an increasing emphasis on multilateral engagement. As a major player in international politics and the world economy, China recognizes the importance of participating in and shaping multilateral institutions and frameworks. In this third part of our discussion on Chinese multilateral engagement, we will explore some key areas where China has been actively involved on the global stage. These areas include trade and economic cooperation, regional security, climate change, and global governance.

Trade and Economic Cooperation

China's economic growth over the past few decades has been nothing short of remarkable, and it has become the world's second-largest economy. As such, trade and economic cooperation are crucial areas of Chinese multilateral engagement. China has been an active participant in various multilateral forums and organizations, including the World Trade Organization (WTO), the G20, and the Asia-Pacific Economic Cooperation (APEC) forum.

Within the WTO, China has sought to strengthen its position as a global economic power and has been actively involved in negotiations on trade liberalization, market access, and dispute settlement. China's accession to the WTO in 2001 marked a significant milestone in its integration into the global trading system. Since then, China has been both a beneficiary and a target of international trade rules, which have shaped its economic policies and practices.

China's participation in the G20, a forum that brings together the world's major economies, has allowed it to play a significant role in shaping global economic governance. As an influential member, China has actively advocated for reforms in the international financial system, such as the inclusion of the Chinese currency, the renminbi, in the International Monetary Fund's (IMF) Special Drawing Rights basket.

Furthermore, China has been actively promoting regional economic integration through initiatives like the Belt and Road Initiative (BRI). The BRI aims to enhance connectivity and trade among countries along the ancient Silk Road routes, encompassing a vast network of infrastructure projects, investments, and trade agreements. Through the BRI, China seeks to foster economic cooperation, expand its market access, and deepen its influence in regions beyond its borders.

Regional Security

China's rising power and growing military capabilities have also led to its increased engagement in regional security affairs. As a key player in the Asia-Pacific region, China has participated in various multilateral security dialogues and mechanisms, such as the Shanghai Cooperation Organization (SCO), the ASEAN Regional Forum (ARF), and the Conference on Interaction and Confidence-Building Measures in Asia (CICA).

The SCO, founded in 2001, is a regional security organization that includes China, Russia, and Central Asian countries. It focuses on promoting security, economic cooperation, and cultural exchanges among its member states. China has actively contributed to the SCO's efforts in combating terrorism, separatism, and extremism, and has sought to strengthen regional stability through enhanced cooperation and dialogue.

China's engagement in the ARF, an ASEAN-led multilateral forum, is aimed at promoting security dialogue and cooperation in the Asia-Pacific region. China has been actively involved in discussions on regional security challenges, such as territorial disputes in the South China Sea, and has advocated for a peaceful resolution based on negotiations and consultations.

CICA, initiated by Kazakhstan in 1992, is another multilateral security mechanism in which China actively participates. It provides a platform for dialogue and confidence-building measures among Asian countries, addressing issues related to security, stability, and cooperation. China's involvement in CICA reflects its commitment to promoting peace, stability, and mutual trust in the region.

Climate Change

Climate change is a global challenge that requires collective efforts, and China has recognized the need for multilateral cooperation to address this issue. As the world's largest emitter of greenhouse gases, China's role in climate change mitigation and adaptation is of crucial importance.

China has been an active participant in multilateral efforts to combat climate change, including the United Nations Framework Convention on Climate Change (UNFCCC) and the Paris Agreement. China ratified the Paris Agreement in 2016 and has made significant commitments to reduce its carbon emissions and promote sustainable development.

Through its domestic policies, China has embarked on an ambitious agenda to transition towards a greener and more sustainable economy. It has set targets to peak its carbon emissions by 2030 and achieve carbon neutrality by 2060. China has also invested heavily in renewable energy, such as solar and wind power, and has become the world's leading producer and consumer of renewable energy technologies.

In addition to domestic efforts, China has been actively engaged in international climate negotiations. It has participated in the annual

UNFCCC Conference of the Parties (COP) meetings, where countries come together to discuss and negotiate climate-related policies and actions. China has advocated for common but differentiated responsibilities, emphasizing the historical emissions of developed countries and the need for financial and technological support to developing countries.

China's multilateral engagement on climate change extends beyond the UNFCCC process. It has launched initiatives like the South-South Cooperation on Climate Change, which aims to promote cooperation and capacity-building among developing countries. China has also played a leading role in the establishment of the Asian Infrastructure Investment Bank (AIIB) and the Green Climate Fund (GCF), both of which support climate-related projects and initiatives.

Global Governance

China's growing influence in global affairs has prompted its increased engagement in global governance institutions and mechanisms. It seeks to shape international norms, rules, and institutions in a manner that aligns with its own interests and priorities. China has been an active participant in multilateral organizations such as the United Nations (UN), the World Bank, and the IMF.

Within the UN, China has sought to expand its influence and contribute to global governance across various domains. It has been a permanent member of the UN Security Council since its establishment, giving it significant decision-making power on matters of international peace and security. China has also increased its contributions to UN peacekeeping operations, becoming one of the largest troop contributors among the permanent members.

China's engagement in global governance extends to the economic sphere as well. It has sought reforms in international financial institutions like the World Bank and the IMF to better reflect the changing global economic landscape. China has also established its own development banks, such as the Asian Infrastructure Investment Bank (AIIB) and the New Development Bank (NDB), to provide alternative sources of financing for infrastructure projects in developing countries.

Moreover, China has been actively involved in shaping global governance in emerging areas such as cyberspace and digital technologies. It has advocated for the concept of "cyber sovereignty," asserting the right of states to govern and regulate the internet within their borders. China has also promoted the development of international norms and standards for emerging technologies, such as artificial intelligence and 5G, through initiatives like the Global Partnership on Artificial Intelligence (GPAI).

China's increasing engagement in multilateralism reflects its growing role as a global power. From trade and economic cooperation to regional security, climate change, and global governance, China has actively participated in various multilateral forums and initiatives. Its involvement aims to protect its interests, shape international norms, and contribute to global governance. As China continues to rise as a major player on the global stage, its multilateral engagement will play a significant role in shaping the future of international relations and cooperation.

Economic Multilateralism: Promoting Cooperation for Global Prosperity

Economic multilateralism is an essential framework that fosters cooperation and collaboration among nations to address global economic challenges and promote shared prosperity. In an increasingly interconnected and interdependent world, where economic activities transcend national borders, multilateralism provides a platform for countries to engage in dialogue, negotiate agreements, and develop collective solutions to address complex economic issues.

This introduction aims to provide a comprehensive overview of economic multilateralism, its historical evolution, key principles, and the significance of multilateral institutions in facilitating global economic cooperation. It will also explore the benefits and challenges associated with economic multilateralism and examine notable examples of multilateral initiatives and organizations.

Historical Evolution of Economic Multilateralism:

The roots of economic multilateralism can be traced back to the aftermath of World War II when nations recognized the need for a cooperative approach to rebuild war-torn economies and prevent future conflicts. The establishment of the Bretton Woods institutions, namely the International Monetary Fund (IMF) and the World Bank, marked a significant milestone in the development of economic multilateralism. These institutions aimed to promote stability, economic growth, and poverty reduction through international financial cooperation.

Following the success of the Bretton Woods institutions, other multilateral organizations emerged, such as the General Agreement on Tariffs and Trade (GATT), which eventually transformed into the World Trade Organization (WTO). The WTO plays a crucial role in facilitating trade negotiations, resolving disputes, and promoting the liberalization of global trade.

Principles of Economic Multilateralism:
Economic multilateralism is guided by several fundamental principles that underpin its functioning and objectives:

a.   Equality   and   Non-discrimination: Multilateralism emphasizes equal treatment and non-discrimination among nations, aiming to create a level playing field in global economic interactions. It seeks to ensure that countries have fair access to markets, resources, and opportunities, regardless of their size or level of development.

b. Cooperation and Collective Decision-making: Multilateralism promotes cooperation among nations and encourages them to work collectively to address common economic challenges. It recognizes that collective decision-making processes involving all stakeholders lead to better outcomes and enhance the legitimacy of international economic governance.

c. Rules-based System: Economic multilateralism relies on a rules-based system to regulate economic interactions between nations. These rules provide a framework for trade, investment, finance, and other economic activities, ensuring predictability, transparency, and stability in the global economic order.

d. Mutual Benefit: The principle of mutual benefit highlights that economic multilateralism should be a win-win proposition, where all participating nations derive benefits from cooperation. By embracing shared gains, countries can foster sustainable economic growth and development for themselves and the global community.

Significance of Multilateral Institutions:

Multilateral institutions play a pivotal role in promoting economic multilateralism. These organizations serve as platforms for dialogue, negotiation, and cooperation, providing a space for countries to discuss and resolve economic issues collectively. They facilitate the exchange of ideas, expertise, and best practices, fostering mutual understanding and trust among nations.

Moreover, multilateral institutions contribute to the development of international norms, standards, and regulations that govern economic activities. They provide technical assistance, capacity-building programs, and policy advice to support member countries in achieving their economic objectives. By promoting policy coordination and coherence, multilateral institutions enhance the efficiency and effectiveness of global economic governance.

Benefits of Economic Multilateralism:

a. Enhanced Market Access: Multilateral trade agreements, such as those negotiated under the auspices of the WTO, reduce barriers to trade, leading to increased market access for goods and services. This expansion of trade opportunities can stimulate economic growth, foster innovation and competitiveness, and generate employment opportunities.

b.   Stability   and   Predictability: Multilateral institutions provide a stable and predictable environment for economic interactions. Through the establishment of rules and dispute settlement mechanisms, they reduce uncertainty and mitigate the risks associated with unilateral actions, protectionism, and trade conflicts. This stability fosters business confidence, encourages investment, and promotes long-term economic growth.

c.   Addressing Global Challenges: Economic multilateralism enables countries to collectively address pressing global challenges that transcend national borders. Issues such as climate change, poverty, inequality, and financial crises require coordinated efforts and joint solutions. Multilateral institutions provide platforms for cooperation, knowledge sharing, and the pooling of resources to tackle these complex challenges effectively.

d. Capacity Building and Development: Multilateral institutions support capacity-building efforts in developing countries by providing technical assistance, financial resources, and knowledge transfer. This assistance helps build institutional capabilities, enhance infrastructure, and foster human capital development, leading to sustainable economic growth and poverty reduction.

e. Fostering Peace and Stability: Economic multilateralism contributes to the promotion of peace and stability among nations. By fostering economic interdependence and cooperation, it reduces the likelihood of conflicts driven by economic rivalries. Through economic integration and mutual benefits, multilateralism strengthens diplomatic ties and encourages peaceful resolution of disputes.

Challenges and Criticisms of Economic Multilateralism:

Despite its significant benefits, economic multilateralism also faces various challenges and criticisms:

a. Power Imbalances: Power imbalances among countries can hinder effective multilateral cooperation. Developed countries often exert greater influence in decision-making processes and shape global economic rules in their favor, while developing countries may face challenges in having their voices and interests adequately represented.

b. Slow Decision-making and Negotiations: Multilateral negotiations can be complex and time-consuming, often involving numerous stakeholders with diverging interests. The consensus-based decision-making processes may result in delays and compromises that impede timely responses to emerging economic issues.

c. Rising Protectionism: The resurgence of protectionist sentiments and unilateral trade actions pose challenges to economic multilateralism. Some countries resort to protectionist measures, such as tariffs and trade barriers, in an attempt to shield domestic industries, which undermines the principles of free trade and hampers global economic integration.

d. Coordination and Implementation Challenges: Implementing multilateral agreements at the national level requires coordination and domestic policy adjustments. The diverse economic and political contexts of member countries can present challenges in aligning domestic policies with multilateral commitments, leading to implementation gaps and limited effectiveness.

e. Lack of Inclusivity: Economic multilateralism needs to ensure inclusivity and participation of all countries, particularly developing nations, to promote equitable outcomes. The concerns and interests of marginalized and vulnerable populations should be addressed to avoid exacerbating inequalities and socioeconomic disparities.

Notable Examples of Economic Multilateralism:

a. The Paris Agreement: The Paris Agreement on climate change, adopted in 2015, exemplifies multilateral efforts to address a global challenge. It establishes a framework for countries to work together to mitigate greenhouse gas emissions, adapt to the effects of climate change, and support sustainable development.

b. Regional Trade Agreements: Regional trade agreements, such as the European Union (EU) and the Association of Southeast Asian Nations (ASEAN), exemplify regional economic multilateralism. These agreements promote economic integration, facilitate trade and investment flows, and contribute to regional stability and prosperity.

c. Sustainable Development Goals (SDGs): The SDGs, adopted by the United Nations in 2015, provide a comprehensive framework for global development cooperation. The SDGs emphasize the importance of economic multilateralism in achieving inclusive and sustainable economic growth, eradicating poverty, and addressing social and environmental challenges.

d. G20 Summits: The Group of Twenty (G20) is an international forum comprising the world's major economies, representing around 85% of global GDP. The G20 brings together leaders to address key economic issues and promote multilateral cooperation. Through the G20, countries collaborate on topics such as financial stability, trade, investment, and development, with the aim of fostering global economic growth and stability.

e. Development Assistance: Multilateral organizations, including the World Bank and regional development banks, play a vital role in providing development assistance to countries in need. These institutions provide financial resources, technical expertise, and policy advice to support poverty reduction, infrastructure development, and capacity building, contributing to inclusive and sustainable economic growth.

Future Prospects and Conclusion:

Economic multilateralism will continue to be a critical framework for addressing global economic challenges and promoting shared prosperity. As the world becomes increasingly interconnected, the need for collaboration and collective action becomes more evident. However, the effectiveness and relevance of economic multilateralism will depend on addressing existing challenges and adapting to evolving dynamics.

To enhance the effectiveness of economic multilateralism, efforts should be made to strengthen inclusivity, promote the participation of developing countries, and address power imbalances in decision-making processes. Streamlining decision-making mechanisms, enhancing transparency, and improving the efficiency of negotiations will contribute to the agility and responsiveness of multilateral institutions.

Moreover, economic multilateralism should be complemented by regional initiatives and bilateral agreements to address specific economic challenges and leverage regional dynamics effectively. Regional integration efforts can promote deeper economic cooperation, harmonize regulations, and stimulate trade and investment flows within specific geographic areas.

In conclusion, economic multilateralism is a vital framework for promoting cooperation, stability, and sustainable economic growth in an interconnected world. By embracing the principles of equality, cooperation, and mutual benefit, multilateral institutions play a crucial role in addressing global economic challenges and fostering shared prosperity. While facing challenges, economic multilateralism remains a powerful mechanism to shape a more inclusive, resilient, and prosperous global economy. Continued commitment to strengthening multilateral cooperation will be essential in navigating the complex economic landscape of the future.

China's Trade and Investment Policies: An Overview of Opportunities and Challenges

China's emergence as a global economic powerhouse has been one of the defining trends of the 21st century. With a population of over 1.4 billion and a rapidly growing middle class, China presents an enormous market potential for businesses around the world. However, understanding China's trade and investment policies is crucial for companies and governments alike to navigate the complexities and seize the opportunities that the Chinese market offers.

This introductory essay aims to provide a comprehensive overview of China's trade and investment policies, shedding light on their historical development, key components, and their implications for the global economy. We will explore the driving forces behind China's trade and investment strategies, examine the policy frameworks that govern these activities, and discuss the challenges and opportunities they present.

Historical Context:
China's trade and investment policies have evolved significantly over the past few decades. The country's economic transformation, which began with market-oriented reforms in the late 1970s, propelled China to become the world's largest exporter and the second-largest economy. We will delve into the historical context of China's policies,

including its accession to the World Trade Organization (WTO) in 2001 and the subsequent integration into the global trading system.

Key Components of China's Trade and Investment Policies:

a. Export-Oriented Economy: China's trade policies have focused on promoting exports as a key driver of economic growth. We will examine the various measures China has implemented to enhance its export competitiveness, such as export subsidies, tax incentives, and infrastructure development.

b. Foreign Direct Investment (FDI): China has also actively sought foreign investment to fuel its economic development. We will explore the policies and regulations governing FDI in China, including the establishment of special economic zones, technology transfer requirements, and intellectual property protection.

c. Free Trade Agreements (FTAs): **China has engaged in regional and bilateral trade agreements to expand market access and promote economic integration. We will discuss China's participation in major FTAs, such as the Regional Comprehensive Economic Partnership (RCEP) and the Belt and Road Initiative (BRI), and their implications for trade and investment flows.**

d. Intellectual Property Rights (IPR): **Intellectual property protection has been a contentious issue in China's trade relations with other countries. We will examine China's efforts to strengthen IPR enforcement, including the establishment of specialized IP courts and revisions to its legal framework.**

Belt and Road Initiative (BRI):

The BRI is China's flagship foreign policy initiative, aiming to enhance connectivity and promote trade and investment between China and countries across Asia, Europe, Africa, and beyond. We will provide an overview of the BRI's objectives, its key infrastructure projects, and the challenges and opportunities it presents for participating countries and the global economy.

Implications for the Global Economy:

a. Global Supply Chains: China's role as the "world's factory" has led to its integration into global supply chains. We will discuss the implications of China's trade policies for global supply chains, including the diversification efforts prompted by trade tensions and the COVID-19 pandemic.

b. Geopolitical Dynamics: China's trade and investment policies have geopolitical implications. We will examine the geopolitical dimensions of China's economic rise, including its relations with major powers like the United States, as well as its influence in international organizations.

c. Environmental and Social Considerations: China's economic growth has come at a cost to the environment and social welfare. We will explore the efforts China has made to address these concerns, such as transitioning to a greener economy and improving labor standards, and their impact on global sustainability.

Challenges and Opportunities:

a. Market Access and Fair Trade: China's trade policies have faced criticism for limiting market access and engaging in unfair trade practices. We will discuss the challenges faced by foreign companies in accessing the Chinese market, including non-tariff barriers, intellectual property infringement, and lack of transparency. Additionally, we will analyze the ongoing trade disputes between China and other major economies, such as the United States, and the potential implications for global trade relations.

b. Technology Transfer and Innovation: China's trade and investment policies have been associated with concerns regarding forced technology transfer and intellectual property theft. We will explore the challenges and opportunities for technology transfer and innovation in the context of China's policies, including the development of domestic technological capabilities and the promotion of indigenous innovation.

c. Risk and Uncertainty: Investing in China comes with inherent risks and uncertainties. We will examine the regulatory environment, legal challenges, and political considerations that companies face when operating in China. We will also discuss strategies for managing risks and navigating the complex business landscape.

d. Market Opportunities: Despite the challenges, China continues to offer significant market opportunities for businesses around the world. We will highlight sectors and industries with high growth potential in China, such as e-commerce, renewable energy, healthcare, and consumer goods, and discuss strategies for entering and succeeding in the Chinese market.

China's trade and investment policies have played a pivotal role in shaping its economic development and its integration into the global economy. Understanding these policies is essential for businesses, governments, and policymakers to navigate the opportunities and challenges presented by the Chinese market. This introduction has provided a comprehensive overview of China's trade and investment policies, covering their historical context, key components, implications for the global economy, and the challenges and opportunities they present. As China's role in the global economy continues to evolve, it is crucial to monitor and analyze its trade and investment policies to make informed decisions and forge mutually beneficial relationships with the world's second-largest economy.

China's Role in Global Economic Governance

The rise of China as a global economic powerhouse has transformed the dynamics of the global economy and reshaped the landscape of global economic governance. As the world's second-largest economy, China's economic policies, trade practices, and financial influence have significant implications for the stability and functioning of the international economic system. Over the past few decades, China has actively engaged in various global economic institutions and initiatives, challenging the traditional dominance of Western powers and contributing to the evolving nature of global economic governance. This essay aims to provide a comprehensive analysis of China's role in global economic governance, examining its involvement in international organizations, its influence on global economic rules and norms, and the implications of its rise for the existing global economic order.

China's Engagement in International Economic Organizations

China's participation in international economic organizations has been instrumental in shaping global economic governance. One of the key organizations in which China plays a significant role is the World Trade Organization (WTO). Since its accession in 2001, China has become an active participant in the multilateral trading system and has contributed to the ongoing negotiations and rulemaking processes. China's growing economic power has enabled it to assert its interests and push for reforms within the WTO framework. For instance, China has advocated for a more balanced approach to trade rules, emphasizing the need for greater inclusivity and development-oriented policies that address the concerns of developing countries.

Apart from the WTO, China has also sought to enhance its influence in regional economic organizations. The establishment of the Asian Infrastructure Investment Bank (AIIB) in 2016 marked a significant milestone in China's efforts to reshape global economic governance. The AIIB, proposed by China and supported by numerous countries, aims to provide financial support for infrastructure development in Asia and beyond. By creating this institution, China has challenged the existing dominance of Western-led financial institutions such as the World Bank and the International Monetary Fund (IMF) and sought to establish a more inclusive and representative international financial architecture.

China's Impact on Global Economic Rules and Norms

China's rise as an economic power has brought about a shift in global economic rules and norms. Traditionally, Western countries have played a leading role in setting the rules and standards for global trade and investment. However, China's growing economic clout and its promotion of alternative models, such as state-led capitalism and industrial policies, have challenged the Western-led economic orthodoxy.

One area where China has sought to shape global economic rules is in the realm of intellectual property rights (IPR). As a major producer and consumer of intellectual property, China's approach to IPR protection has been a subject of contention. Critics argue that China's lax enforcement of IPR laws has allowed for widespread infringement and unfair competition. However, China has taken steps to strengthen its IPR regime and has become more active in international discussions on IPR standards. Its engagement in global forums has led to the incorporation of some of its concerns, such as the need for a balanced approach to IPR protection that considers the developmental needs of emerging economies.

Furthermore, China's Belt and Road Initiative (BRI) has had a profound impact on global economic governance. The BRI, launched in 2013, aims to enhance connectivity and promote economic cooperation across Asia, Europe, and Africa. By financing infrastructure projects in participating countries, China has sought to create a network of economic relationships that align with its interests. The BRI's scale and scope have raised concerns about debt sustainability, environmental impacts, and potential geopolitical implications. However, China has responded to criticisms by emphasizing the need for transparency, sustainability, and inclusive development in BRI projects.

Implications of China's Rise for Global Economic Order

China's ascent as a global economic power has raised questions about the future trajectory of the existing global economic order. Its growing influence and alternative approaches to economic governance have led to both opportunities and challenges for the international community.

One of the key implications of China's rise is the shifting power dynamics in global economic governance. Historically, Western powers, particularly the United States, have dominated global economic institutions and decision-making processes. However, China's economic might and assertive stance have challenged this dominance and led to a more multipolar world order. As China's economic influence continues to grow, it is likely to exert greater influence over global economic governance, potentially leading to a rebalancing of power and decision-making structures.

China's rise also presents opportunities for developing countries. With its emphasis on development-oriented policies and inclusivity,

China has positioned itself as a champion of South-South cooperation and a potential alternative to Western-led economic institutions. Through initiatives like the AIIB and the BRI, China has provided much-needed infrastructure funding and investment to countries in Africa, Asia, and beyond. This has allowed developing nations to diversify their funding sources and reduce their dependence on traditional Western institutions. However, concerns remain about debt sustainability and the long-term implications of China's economic engagement in these regions.

Another implication of China's rise is the potential for greater economic integration in the Asia-Pacific region. China's economic clout has facilitated the deepening of economic ties with neighboring countries through initiatives like the Regional Comprehensive Economic Partnership (RCEP) and the Free Trade Area of the Asia-Pacific (FTAAP). These agreements aim to reduce trade barriers and promote economic integration among participating nations. As China's economic relationships strengthen in the region, it is likely to shape the future of regional economic governance and potentially challenge the dominance of Western-led trade arrangements.

However, China's growing influence also raises concerns about its commitment to global economic norms and standards. Critics argue that China's state-led economic model and its industrial policies, such as subsidies for domestic industries, create unfair advantages and distort global markets. Furthermore, China's human rights record, restrictions on foreign investment, and limited market access have been subjects of criticism. As China assumes a greater role in global economic governance, there is a need for increased transparency, adherence to international rules, and the inclusion of all stakeholders in decision-making processes.

The rise of China also poses challenges to the existing global economic architecture. The traditional Western-led institutions, such as the IMF and the World Bank, were established in a post-World War II era when Western powers held economic and political dominance. China's economic ascent calls into question the legitimacy and effectiveness of these institutions in addressing the needs and interests of emerging economies. This has prompted calls for reform and greater representation of developing countries in global economic decision-making.

In conclusion, China's role in global economic governance has undergone significant transformation in recent decades. As the world's second-largest economy, China's engagement in international economic organizations, its impact on global economic rules and norms, and its rise as a global economic power have reshaped the dynamics of the global economic order. While China's rise presents opportunities for developing countries and has led to a more multipolar world, it also raises concerns about its commitment to global economic norms, transparency, and inclusivity. As China's influence continues to grow, finding a balance between accommodating its interests and ensuring a fair and equitable global economic order will be crucial for the international community.

Chinese-Led Economic Initiatives: Exploring the RCEP and CPTPP

In an era of interconnectedness and global trade, economic initiatives play a crucial role in shaping the future of nations and their economies. Two significant initiatives that have gained immense attention in recent years are the Regional Comprehensive Economic Partnership (RCEP) and the Comprehensive and Progressive Agreement for Trans-Pacific Partnership (CPTPP). As both initiatives have Chinese leadership or involvement, they have emerged as key drivers of economic integration and cooperation in the Asia-Pacific region. In this introductory essay, we will delve into the RCEP and CPTPP, exploring their origins, objectives, significance, and potential impact on regional and global trade dynamics.

Background:

1.1 Global Trade and Economic Integration:

The 21st century has witnessed an exponential growth in global trade, accompanied by increased interconnectivity and interdependence among nations. Economic integration has become a vital tool for countries to enhance competitiveness, stimulate growth, and promote cooperation. Various regional and bilateral trade agreements have been established worldwide to facilitate cross-border trade and investment.

1.2 Chinese Leadership and Ambitions:

China, as the world's second-largest economy and a major global trade player, has taken a proactive approach to enhance its economic influence and regional connectivity. Under President Xi Jinping's leadership, China has launched several ambitious economic initiatives to bolster its economic partnerships and exert greater influence on the global stage. The RCEP and CPTPP are among the most prominent initiatives pursued by China in recent years.

The Regional Comprehensive Economic Partnership (RCEP):

2.1 Origins and Negotiations:

The RCEP is a free trade agreement (FTA) negotiation that originated in 2012, primarily led by the Association of Southeast Asian Nations (ASEAN) along with six dialogue partners: China, Japan, South Korea, Australia, New Zealand, and India. The negotiations aimed to create an integrated economic bloc that encompasses almost half of the world's population and accounts for about one-third of global GDP.

2.2 Objectives and Scope:

The RCEP aims to eliminate tariffs and non-tariff barriers, promote investment flows, enhance intellectual property rights protection, and facilitate economic cooperation among its member countries. By establishing a common set of rules and reducing trade barriers, the RCEP seeks to foster economic growth, promote regional supply chains, and enhance the overall competitiveness of its member economies.

2.3 Significance and Implications:

The RCEP's significance lies in its potential to reshape global trade patterns and enhance economic integration in the Asia-Pacific region. With China as a key participant, the RCEP is seen as a counterweight to the influence of Western-led economic initiatives such as the Trans Pacific Partnership (TPP) and the United States-Mexico-Canada Agreement (USMCA). The RCEP's inclusion of India, although it has withdrawn from the agreement, highlights the scope and ambition of this economic integration effort.

The Comprehensive and Progressive Agreement for Trans-Pacific Partnership (CPTPP):

3.1 Origins and Evolution:

The CPTPP, originally known as the TPP, was a trade agreement initiated by the United States in 2005 with the aim of deepening economic integration among the Asia-Pacific nations. However, the U.S. withdrew from the agreement in 2017, prompting the remaining 11 member countries to negotiate a revised version known as the CPTPP.

3.2 Objectives and Scope:

The CPTPP seeks to establish a high-standard, comprehensive trade agreement among its member countries, which include Australia, Brunei, Canada, Chile, Japan, Malaysia, Mexico, New Zealand, Peru,

Singapore, and Vietnam. The agreement aims to reduce tariffs, enhance regulatory coherence, promote investment flows, protect intellectual property rights, and address various non-tariff barriers. The CPTPP also includes provisions related to labor rights, environmental protection, and dispute settlement mechanisms.

3.3 Significance and Implications:
The CPTPP holds significant implications for regional and global trade dynamics. With the United States' withdrawal, the agreement took on a new form, but its core objectives remained intact. The CPTPP has been seen as a way for member countries to diversify their trade and reduce reliance on any single market. It also serves as a signal of commitment to open and rules-based trade, promoting economic integration and cooperation among its member nations.

Comparative Analysis:

4.1 Overlapping Membership:

One notable aspect of both the RCEP and CPTPP is the presence of overlapping membership. Several countries, including Japan, Australia, New Zealand, and Vietnam, are part of both agreements. This overlapping membership highlights the complex dynamics of economic integration in the Asia-Pacific region and the efforts of countries to balance their economic relationships with different partners.

4.2 Differences in Scope and Ambitions:

While both initiatives aim to promote economic integration and cooperation, there are notable differences in their scope and ambitions. The RCEP, with its larger membership and broader regional coverage, seeks to establish a comprehensive economic bloc that addresses a wide range of trade and investment issues. On the other hand, the CPTPP, with its smaller membership but higher standards, focuses on establishing a high-quality trade agreement that sets rigorous rules and regulations for its members.

4.3 Chinese Leadership and Influence:

China's role as a key participant in both initiatives cannot be overlooked. With its economic might and regional influence, China has played a significant role in shaping the direction and outcomes of these economic initiatives. The Chinese-led RCEP reflects China's vision of an integrated regional economy under its leadership, while its involvement in the CPTPP showcases its efforts to actively engage in trade liberalization even outside its immediate sphere of influence.

Potential Impact:

5.1 Regional Trade and Investment Flows:

The RCEP and CPTPP have the potential to significantly impact regional trade and investment flows. By reducing trade barriers and harmonizing regulations, these agreements can stimulate cross-border economic activities and promote the growth of regional supply chains. They also provide a platform for member countries to attract foreign direct investment, foster technology transfer, and enhance market access.

5.2 Influence on Global Trade Architecture:
The emergence of the RCEP and CPTPP has the potential to reshape the global trade architecture. As China takes a leading role in economic initiatives, it challenges the traditional dominance of Western-led trade agreements. The RCEP, with its vast membership and economic significance, has the potential to become a major force in shaping regional trade dynamics. The CPTPP, despite the absence of the United States, still holds considerable influence and can contribute to the development of new trade norms and standards.

5.3 Geopolitical Implications:
The RCEP and CPTPP also have geopolitical implications. These initiatives provide an avenue

for countries to enhance their economic ties, build strategic alliances, and strengthen regional cooperation. They can shape the geopolitical landscape by fostering closer relationships among member countries and potentially shifting the balance of power in the Asia-Pacific region.

The Chinese-led economic initiatives, the RCEP and CPTPP, have emerged as significant drivers of economic integration and cooperation in the Asia-Pacific region. With their ambitious objectives, these agreements aim to foster trade liberalization, promote investment flows, and enhance economic connectivity. Their potential impact on regional and global trade dynamics, as well as their geopolitical implications, cannot be underestimated. As these initiatives continue to evolve, it is essential to closely monitor their implementation and assess their outcomes in order to understand their effectiveness in achieving their intended goals and the implications for participating countries and the wider international community. The RCEP and

CPTPP represent two distinct approaches to economic integration, with the RCEP emphasizing inclusivity and regional coverage, and the CPTPP focusing on higher standards and regulatory coherence. The overlapping membership of several countries underscores the complex web of economic relationships and the desire to diversify trade partnerships. China's involvement in both initiatives highlights its growing influence in shaping regional economic architecture.

Looking ahead, the successful implementation of the RCEP and CPTPP will depend on several factors. Member countries must navigate the challenges of harmonizing regulations, addressing non-tariff barriers, and ensuring equitable distribution of benefits. Additionally, active participation and adherence to the agreed-upon rules and commitments are crucial for the effective functioning of these agreements. Robust enforcement mechanisms, such as dispute settlement procedures, will play a vital role in maintaining the credibility and integrity of these economic initiatives.

The RCEP and CPTPP also face external challenges and uncertainties. Geopolitical tensions, changes in leadership, and shifts in global trade policies can impact the progress and dynamics of these agreements. It remains to be seen how these initiatives will coexist with existing regional and global trade frameworks, such as the World Trade Organization (WTO), and whether they will contribute to the fragmentation or convergence of international trade rules and standards.

Furthermore, the COVID-19 pandemic has presented both opportunities and challenges for the RCEP and CPTPP. The pandemic has disrupted global supply chains, exposed vulnerabilities in trade networks, and highlighted the importance of resilience and adaptability. These economic initiatives can serve as platforms for post-pandemic recovery and reconfiguration of supply chains, promoting regional economic cooperation and stability.

Security Multilateralism

In today's interconnected world, the security landscape is evolving rapidly, necessitating the need for robust multilateral approaches to address emerging threats. Security multilateralism refers to the cooperative efforts among multiple nations to collectively tackle security challenges through shared goals, norms, and institutions. China, as a rising global power, plays a significant role in shaping the dynamics of security multilateralism. This introductory essay aims to explore China's defense and security policies and their impact on security multilateralism.

China's Emergence as a Global Power:

Over the past few decades, China has experienced remarkable economic growth, transforming itself into the world's second-largest economy. This rise in economic prowess has enabled China to expand its political influence and military capabilities. As a result, China's defense and security policies have garnered international attention, raising questions about its intentions and the implications for security multilateralism.

China's National Security Concept:

China's national security concept has undergone significant changes in recent years. Historically, China adopted a defensive posture and focused on maintaining internal stability and territorial integrity. However, as China's global interests expanded, its security concept has evolved to include a more proactive approach. The current concept emphasizes a comprehensive security framework that encompasses both traditional and non-traditional security threats.

Modernization of the Chinese Military:

China's military modernization has been a central element of its defense and security policies. The Chinese People's Liberation Army (PLA) has undergone significant reforms aimed at enhancing its capabilities across various domains, including air, sea, space, and cyberspace. The development of advanced weapon systems, such as aircraft carriers, stealth fighters, and hypersonic missiles, has increased China's power projection capabilities and influence in regional security dynamics.

Regional Security Challenges:

China's expanding military capabilities have raised concerns among its neighbors and other major powers. In the Asia-Pacific region, territorial disputes in the South China Sea and East China Sea have strained regional relations, leading to heightened tensions. China's assertive actions, such as island-building and increasing military presence in disputed areas, have generated security dilemmas and fueled the need for multilateral approaches to address these challenges.

China's Belt and Road Initiative (BRI):

China's ambitious Belt and Road Initiative (BRI) has emerged as a major component of its foreign policy and regional engagement. BRI aims to enhance connectivity and economic cooperation through infrastructure development across Asia, Africa, Europe, and beyond. While BRI offers potential economic benefits, it also presents security implications. The initiative's vast scale and China's growing influence in recipient countries raise questions about debt dependency, transparency, and potential military implications.

China's Participation in Security Multilateralism:

China's engagement in security multilateralism has been a subject of considerable debate. On one hand, China has actively participated in various regional and international security mechanisms, such as the Shanghai Cooperation Organization (SCO), the ASEAN Regional Forum (ARF), and the United Nations peacekeeping operations. These engagements demonstrate China's willingness to contribute to global security and stability.

On the other hand, China's approach to multilateralism has been characterized by a mix of cooperation and assertiveness. China's territorial disputes in the South China Sea and its resistance to international arbitration rulings have strained its relationships with neighboring countries and raised concerns about its commitment to international norms and rules-based order. China's expanding military capabilities, coupled with its growing influence, have led to debates about its intentions and the potential for a power shift in global security dynamics.

Implications for Security Multilateralism:

China's defense and security policies have profound implications for security multilateralism. Its rising power challenges the existing order and tests the resilience of multilateral institutions. China's emphasis on sovereignty and non-interference raises questions about its willingness to align with international norms and standards. This divergence in approaches can create tensions and hinder effective cooperation within multilateral frameworks.

One key aspect of China's impact on security multilateralism is its role as a veto-wielding member of the United Nations Security Council (UNSC). As a permanent member, China's stance on various security issues, such as conflict resolution, sanctions, and peacekeeping operations, significantly influences global security decision-making. China's positions often reflect its national interests and may not always align with those of other major powers or regional actors. This can impede consensus-building and compromise within the UNSC, making it challenging to address complex security challenges effectively.

China's Belt and Road Initiative (BRI) also has implications for security multilateralism. While BRI promotes economic connectivity and development, its vast infrastructure projects have strategic implications. The initiative's expansion into regions of geopolitical significance raises concerns about the potential for China to exert political influence and leverage its economic power for strategic gains. This has led to debates about the need for multilateral oversight and transparency to ensure that BRI projects adhere to international standards and do not undermine the sovereignty and security of recipient countries.

China's growing military capabilities and assertive actions in disputed areas, such as the South China Sea, have triggered regional anxieties and prompted neighboring countries to seek multilateral support. This has resulted in the strengthening of existing security alliances, such as the US-led Indo-Pacific strategy and the Quadrilateral Security Dialogue (Quad), comprising the United States, Japan, Australia, and India. These multilateral frameworks aim to maintain a balance of power and uphold a rules-based order in the region.

Furthermore, China's engagement in regional multilateral mechanisms, such as the Shanghai Cooperation Organization (SCO) and the Association of Southeast Asian Nations (ASEAN), plays a crucial role in shaping security dynamics. China's active involvement in these forums allows it to exert influence and shape the agenda to some extent. However, differences in perspectives and conflicting interests among member states can limit the effectiveness of these multilateral platforms in addressing security challenges.

China's approach to security multilateralism is also intertwined with its broader geopolitical ambitions. As China seeks to expand its influence globally, it has launched initiatives such as the Asian Infrastructure Investment Bank (AIIB) and the Forum on China-Africa Cooperation (FOCAC) to enhance its economic and political ties with various regions. These initiatives provide China with opportunities to shape regional security agendas and influence the multilateral landscape.

However, China's rise as a global power also presents opportunities for enhanced security multilateralism. China has the potential to contribute significantly to global peacekeeping operations, humanitarian assistance, and disaster relief efforts. Its growing military capabilities and economic resources can be harnessed for collective security initiatives, fostering greater cooperation among nations to address common security challenges such as terrorism, cyber threats, and non-proliferation.

To maximize the potential of security multilateralism, it is essential to promote dialogue, trust-building, and mutual understanding between China and other major powers. Constructive engagement and the establishment of mechanisms to manage and mitigate tensions can help build a more inclusive and effective security architecture.

In conclusion, China's defense and security policies have significant implications for security multilateralism. As a rising global power, China's approach to multilateral cooperation, its military modernization, and its expanding regional influence shape the dynamics of global security. China's participation in multilateral mechanisms and its Belt and Road Initiative present both challenges and opportunities for collective security efforts. Navigating the complexities of China's rise requires constructive engagement, dialogue, and the pursuit of shared interests to strengthen security multilateralism and ensure a stable and prosperous global order.

China's Defense and Security Policies: A Comprehensive Analysis

China's emergence as a global power has been accompanied by a significant transformation of its defense and security policies. As the world's most populous nation and the second-largest economy, China's military capabilities and security strategies have far-reaching implications for regional and global stability. Understanding China's defense and security policies is crucial for policymakers, scholars, and international observers seeking to comprehend China's rise and its potential impact on the international order.

This comprehensive analysis aims to provide an in-depth examination of China's defense and security policies. By exploring the historical, political, and strategic factors shaping China's approach, we will delve into key areas such as military modernization, territorial disputes, maritime ambitions, cyber warfare, and nuclear capabilities. Furthermore, we will assess the implications of China's defense and security policies on regional dynamics, great power relations, and global security.

Historical Context:

To comprehend China's defense and security policies, it is essential to consider the historical factors that have shaped its strategic outlook. China has a long history of valuing its territorial integrity and security. The memory of colonial invasions and conflicts, such as the Opium Wars and Japanese aggression, has influenced China's contemporary approach to defense and security. The Chinese Communist Party's rise to power in 1949 and the subsequent establishment of the People's Republic of China (PRC) laid the foundation for China's modern defense establishment.

Policy Framework and Decision-Making:

China's defense and security policies are shaped by a complex policy framework and decision-making process. The Chinese Communist Party's Central Military Commission (CMC) holds ultimate authority over the People's Liberation Army (PLA). The PLA's modernization and strategic planning are guided by documents such as the Defense White Paper, National Defense Law, and military reforms. Understanding China's policy framework and decision-making process is crucial for comprehending its defense and security priorities.

Military Modernization:

China has embarked on an ambitious military modernization drive aimed at transforming the PLA into a modern, technologically advanced force. This process involves significant investments in defense spending, research and development, and the acquisition of advanced weaponry. We will examine China's modernization efforts across its land, air, naval, and cyber domains, assessing their implications for regional power dynamics and the balance of power.

China's territorial disputes, particularly in the East and South China Seas, have garnered significant attention and raised concerns among neighboring countries and the international community. We will explore China's claims over disputed territories, its approach to resolving these disputes, and the potential implications for regional stability. Additionally, we will analyze the role of historical, geopolitical, and resource-related factors in shaping China's territorial ambitions.

China's expanding maritime capabilities and interests have raised questions about its intentions in the Indo-Pacific region and beyond. The PLA Navy's (PLAN) growing blue-water capabilities, naval deployments, and establishment of overseas military bases demonstrate China's maritime ambitions. We will assess China's maritime strategy, its evolving naval doctrine, and the implications for regional security and great power competition.

Cyber Warfare:

China's increasing reliance on cyberspace for economic, military, and political purposes has raised concerns about its cyber warfare capabilities and intentions. China has been accused of engaging in state-sponsored cyber espionage, intellectual property theft, and the development of offensive cyber capabilities. We will explore China's cyber warfare doctrine, its cyber espionage activities, and the challenges it poses to global cybersecurity.

Nuclear Capabilities:

China's nuclear capabilities and its role in the global nuclear order deserve attention in the context of its defense and security policies. We will analyze China's nuclear doctrine, its pursuit of a credible nuclear deterrent, and its impact on

China's Participation in Arms Control and Non-Proliferation

China's participation in arms control and non-proliferation has been a subject of great interest and concern in the international community. As one of the world's major powers and a nuclear-armed state, China's role in maintaining global security and stability is crucial. The country's approach to arms control and non-proliferation has evolved over the years, reflecting its changing security environment, strategic interests, and international responsibilities. This essay aims to provide an in-depth analysis of China's participation in arms control and non-proliferation efforts, examining its historical trajectory, current policy, and future prospects.

Historical Context:

China's engagement with arms control and non-proliferation can be traced back to the early years of the People's Republic of China (PRC). After its establishment in 1949, China pursued an independent foreign policy that aimed to safeguard its sovereignty and national security. During the Cold War, China developed its nuclear weapons program and conducted its first nuclear test in 1964, becoming the fifth nuclear-armed state. However, unlike the United States and the Soviet Union, China maintained a relatively small nuclear arsenal and adopted a policy of minimum deterrence.

China's initial stance towards arms control and non-proliferation was influenced by its revolutionary ideology and the perception of being surrounded by potential adversaries. The country emphasized the principle of "no first use" of nuclear weapons and advocated for complete nuclear disarmament. China joined the Treaty on the Non-Proliferation of Nuclear Weapons (NPT) in 1992, committing to the treaty's goals of disarmament and non-proliferation. It also signed the Comprehensive Nuclear-Test-Ban Treaty (CTBT) in 1996, reinforcing its commitment to nuclear arms control.

Arms Control Agreements:

China's participation in arms control agreements has been limited compared to other nuclear-armed states. The United States and Russia have concluded a series of bilateral agreements, such as the Strategic Arms Reduction Treaty (START), aimed at reducing their nuclear arsenals. In contrast, China's smaller nuclear stockpile and its perception of maintaining a credible deterrent have led it to adopt a cautious approach to arms control negotiations.

China has expressed support for multilateral arms control efforts, particularly within the framework of the United Nations (UN) and the Conference on Disarmament. It has advocated for the complete prohibition and elimination of nuclear weapons, calling for a step-by-step approach to achieve disarmament. However, China has been hesitant to engage in comprehensive arms control agreements, citing concerns about its national security and the disparity in nuclear capabilities between itself and the United States and Russia.

Non-Proliferation Efforts:

As a signatory to the NPT, China is committed to preventing the spread of nuclear weapons and promoting the peaceful use of nuclear energy. It has implemented export control measures to regulate the transfer of sensitive nuclear technology and materials. China has also supported the International Atomic Energy Agency (IAEA) in its efforts to monitor and verify compliance with non-proliferation obligations.

However, China's non-proliferation record has been a subject of debate. Critics argue that China has been too lenient in its approach to countries that have violated non-proliferation norms, such as North Korea and Pakistan. China's historical support for Pakistan's nuclear program and its reluctance to endorse strong sanctions against North Korea have raised concerns about its commitment to non-proliferation.

Emerging Challenges and Opportunities:

China's growing economic and military power, coupled with its expanding global influence, has brought new challenges and opportunities in the realm of arms control and non-proliferation. China's military modernization, including the development of advanced conventional and strategic capabilities, has raised concerns among its neighbors and the United States. These developments have prompted calls for greater transparency and dialogue regarding China's military capabilities and intentions.

In recent years, China has made efforts to enhance its participation in arms control and non-proliferation initiatives. It has participated in various multilateral forums, such as the Proliferation Security Initiative and the Hague Code of Conduct against Ballistic Missile Proliferation, demonstrating its willingness to engage in international non-proliferation efforts. China has also engaged in bilateral dialogues with the United States and other countries on strategic stability and arms control issues.

One notable development is China's participation in the negotiation of the Joint Comprehensive Plan of Action (JCPOA) with Iran in 2015. As a permanent member of the United Nations Security Council, China played a significant role in reaching a diplomatic solution to the Iranian nuclear issue. China's involvement in the JCPOA highlights its commitment to non-proliferation and its growing role as a responsible stakeholder in global security affairs.

China's Belt and Road Initiative (BRI), a vast infrastructure and development project spanning multiple continents, presents both challenges and opportunities for arms control and non-proliferation. Critics argue that the BRI could facilitate the spread of dual-use technologies and weapons to countries with questionable non-proliferation records. However, China has also emphasized the importance of promoting peaceful development and regional stability through the BRI, pledging to adhere to international norms and standards.

China's evolving space program is another area that raises arms control and non-proliferation concerns. As China's space capabilities advance, there are worries about the militarization of space and the potential for an arms race in outer space. China's successful anti-satellite missile test in 2007 and its ongoing development of space-based assets have fueled these concerns. Efforts to establish norms and regulations for responsible behavior in space will be essential to prevent the escalation of tensions.

Looking ahead, there are several key factors that will shape China's participation in arms control and non-proliferation. First, China's evolving security environment will influence its approach. As China faces new challenges and threats, such as territorial disputes and regional tensions, its security concerns may impact its willingness to engage in arms control negotiations. Balancing its national security interests with global disarmament efforts will be a delicate task for Chinese policymakers.

Second, China's relationship with the United States will play a crucial role. The strategic competition between the two countries, particularly in the Asia-Pacific region, has implications for arms control and non-proliferation. Cooperation and trust-building measures between China and the United States will be essential to address shared concerns and promote mutual confidence in the realm of arms control.

Third, China's domestic political dynamics will influence its approach to arms control and non-proliferation. China's leadership and public opinion will shape the country's policies and priorities in this area. As China's middle class expands and its citizens become more engaged in global issues, public pressure for greater transparency and accountability in arms control and non-proliferation may grow.

In conclusion, China's participation in arms control and non-proliferation is a complex and evolving issue. China's historical trajectory, current policies, and future prospects demonstrate a mix of commitment, cautiousness, and competing interests. As a nuclear-armed state and a major global player, China's engagement in arms control and non-proliferation efforts is of utmost importance for global security and stability.

International cooperation, dialogue, and confidence-building measures will be essential to address the challenges and opportunities presented by China's role in this critical area.

Regional Security Cooperation in the Asia-Pacific: A Multilateral Approach to Ensuring Stability and Prosperity

The Asia-Pacific region, with its diverse and rapidly evolving geopolitical landscape, has become a focal point for global attention in recent decades. As home to some of the world's largest economies, emerging powers, and territorial disputes, the region's security dynamics have a significant impact on global stability and prosperity. In light of this, regional security cooperation has emerged as a crucial mechanism for managing and mitigating the challenges and risks that confront the Asia-Pacific.

This introduction aims to provide a comprehensive overview of the concept of regional security cooperation in the Asia-Pacific, examining its historical development, key actors, and evolving dynamics. It explores the underlying motivations for cooperation, the major security challenges faced by the region, and the various multilateral frameworks and initiatives that have been established to foster collaboration and enhance regional security.

Historical Context:

The historical context of regional security cooperation in the Asia-Pacific can be traced back to the aftermath of World War II. The region experienced significant political and economic transformations, leading to the establishment of new nation-states and the reconfiguration of existing power structures. The emergence of the Cold War further exacerbated regional tensions and security dilemmas, which eventually prompted countries to seek mechanisms for collective security.

Motivations for Cooperation:

Cooperation in the Asia-Pacific is driven by several key factors. First and foremost, the region's rapid economic growth and increasing interdependence have created a shared interest in maintaining stability and safeguarding economic prosperity. Moreover, the presence of numerous security challenges, such as territorial disputes, terrorism, proliferation of weapons of mass destruction, and non-traditional security threats, has highlighted the necessity for collective action.

Security Challenges:

The Asia-Pacific region faces a range of complex security challenges that require collaborative responses. These challenges include unresolved territorial disputes, such as the South China Sea dispute, the Korean Peninsula issue, maritime piracy, transnational crime, cybersecurity threats, natural disasters, and pandemics. Addressing these multifaceted challenges necessitates coordinated efforts, as they often transcend national borders and require comprehensive and long-term solutions.

Major Actors:

Several major actors play significant roles in shaping regional security cooperation in the Asia-Pacific. The United States has been a longstanding security guarantor and has actively engaged in various regional security initiatives, such as the Association of Southeast Asian Nations (ASEAN) Regional Forum and the East Asia Summit. China, as an emerging power, has also sought to enhance its role in regional security affairs through initiatives like the Belt and Road Initiative and the Shanghai Cooperation Organization. Other key actors include Japan, India, Australia, South Korea, and ASEAN member states.

To address the complex security challenges, numerous multilateral frameworks and initiatives have been established in the Asia-Pacific region. These frameworks serve as platforms for dialogue, confidence-building, and cooperation among regional states. The ASEAN-centered mechanisms, including the ASEAN Regional Forum, the East Asia Summit, and the ASEAN Defense Ministers' Meeting Plus, have been instrumental in fostering regional security cooperation. Additionally, other initiatives such as the Shanghai Cooperation Organization, the Asia-Pacific Economic Cooperation, and the Quadrilateral Security Dialogue (Quad) have gained prominence in recent years.

Evolving Dynamics:

The dynamics of regional security cooperation in the Asia-Pacific are constantly evolving. The rise of new regional powers, changing geopolitical alignments, and the evolving nature of security threats continue to shape the landscape. The strategic competition between the United States and China, often referred to as the "Indo-Pacific rivalry," has added a new dimension to regional security dynamics. Balancing between great powers and maintaining inclusivity in regional mechanisms remain key challenges.

Future Prospects and Challenges:

Looking ahead, regional Future Prospects and Challenges (continued):

security cooperation in the Asia-Pacific faces both opportunities and challenges. On one hand, there is an increasing recognition among regional states of the need for collaborative approaches to address shared security challenges. The growing economic interdependence and the realization that no single country can tackle complex security issues alone provide an impetus for further cooperation.

On the other hand, there are several challenges that pose obstacles to effective regional security cooperation. One such challenge is the diversity of interests and perspectives among the various actors in the region. Different countries have different priorities, threat perceptions, and historical grievances, which can hinder consensus-building and limit the scope of cooperation.

Another challenge lies in managing power rivalries and competition among major actors. The United States and China, in particular, have competing visions for the region, which can lead to tensions and potential conflicts. Striking a balance between great power competition and cooperation is crucial for maintaining regional stability.

Additionally, the effectiveness and inclusivity of existing multilateral frameworks need to be continually assessed and enhanced. Some frameworks, such as the ASEAN-centered mechanisms, have been criticized for their slow decision-making processes and limited enforcement mechanisms. Strengthening the institutional capacity, transparency, and accountability of these frameworks will be crucial for their long-term effectiveness.

Furthermore, non-traditional security threats, such as cybersecurity, climate change, and pandemics, are increasingly prominent in the Asia-Pacific region. These challenges require new approaches and innovative cooperation mechanisms beyond traditional security frameworks. Strengthening collaboration in areas such as information sharing, capacity building, and joint response mechanisms will be essential to effectively address these evolving threats.

Despite the challenges, there are several avenues for deepening regional security cooperation in the Asia-Pacific. First, enhancing dialogue and communication channels among regional states is vital. Regular dialogues, track-two diplomacy, and confidence-building measures can help build trust and foster greater understanding of each other's perspectives and concerns.

Second, inclusive regional frameworks should be further developed to ensure the participation of all relevant actors. This includes involving not only states but also non-state actors, such as civil society organizations and academia, in discussions and initiatives. Inclusivity can help address the diverse interests and foster a sense of shared ownership in regional security cooperation.

Third, there is a need to strengthen functional cooperation in specific areas of security, such as maritime security, counterterrorism, and disaster response. Developing joint training exercises, information-sharing mechanisms, and capacity-building programs can enhance regional capabilities and promote collaboration on specific security challenges.

Lastly, regional states should explore opportunities for cooperative approaches to address power rivalries and mitigate tensions. Confidence-building measures, transparency in military activities, and crisis management mechanisms can contribute to reducing the risk of miscalculation and escalation.

In conclusion, regional security cooperation in the Asia-Pacific is essential for maintaining stability, peace, and prosperity in a region characterized by diverse interests, complex security challenges, and evolving power dynamics. While there are inherent challenges, the increasing recognition of the importance of collaboration, the existing multilateral frameworks, and the potential for innovative approaches provide a foundation for further enhancing regional security cooperation. By fostering dialogue, inclusivity, functional cooperation, and managing power rivalries, the Asia-Pacific region can navigate the complex security landscape and work towards a more secure and prosperous future.

Climate Change and Environmental Multilateralism: An Introduction

Climate change is one of the most pressing challenges of our time, posing significant threats to the environment, societies, and economies around the world. Its impacts, including rising global temperatures, extreme weather events, sea-level rise, and ecosystem disruptions, are increasingly felt across continents and affect diverse aspects of human life. Recognizing the transboundary nature of this issue, nations have come together to address climate change through multilateral cooperation and agreements. This introduction aims to provide an overview of climate change and the importance of environmental multilateralism in tackling this global crisis.

Understanding Climate Change

1.1. The Science of Climate Change

Climate change refers to long-term shifts in weather patterns and average temperatures on Earth, primarily caused by human activities. The Intergovernmental Panel on Climate Change (IPCC), a leading international body of climate scientists, has provided extensive evidence confirming the role of human activities, particularly the emission of greenhouse gases (GHGs), in driving climate change. The burning of fossil fuels, deforestation, industrial processes, and agricultural practices are major contributors to GHG emissions.

1.2. Impacts of Climate Change

Climate change has far-reaching consequences for ecosystems, biodiversity, and human well-being. It exacerbates natural disasters such as hurricanes, droughts, and wildfires, leading to significant economic losses and the displacement of communities. Rising temperatures affect agriculture, water availability, and public health, increasing the risk of food and water shortages, heat-related illnesses, and the spread of vector-borne diseases. Furthermore, coastal regions are vulnerable to sea-level rise, causing increased coastal erosion, loss of habitats, and threats to infrastructure.

The Need for Multilateral Cooperation

2.1. Transboundary Nature of Climate Change

Climate change does not respect national boundaries, making it a global issue that requires collective action. The emission of GHGs in one country can affect the climate and ecosystems of distant regions, underscoring the interconnectivity of the Earth's systems. As such, addressing climate change necessitates collaboration among nations to mitigate emissions, adapt to its impacts, and develop sustainable solutions.

2.2. Environmental Multilateralism

Multilateralism refers to the principle of organizing relations between nations based on cooperation, collective decision-making, and shared responsibility. Environmental multilateralism specifically focuses on cooperation and coordination among nations to address environmental challenges, including climate change. It involves the negotiation of international agreements, the establishment of institutional frameworks, and the development of common goals and strategies to tackle environmental issues collectively.

Key Milestones in Environmental Multilateralism

3.1. United Nations Framework Convention on Climate Change (UNFCCC)

The UNFCCC, established in 1992, is a landmark international treaty aimed at mitigating climate change and facilitating adaptation. It sets out a framework for multilateral cooperation on climate change, with the objective of stabilizing GHG concentrations in the atmosphere to prevent dangerous anthropogenic interference with the climate system. The UNFCCC's annual Conference of the Parties (COP) brings together representatives from member countries to discuss and negotiate climate-related issues.

3.2. Kyoto Protocol

Adopted in 1997, the Kyoto Protocol is an international agreement under the UNFCCC that commits developed countries to specific GHG emissions reduction targets. It introduced the concept of binding emissions targets and established mechanisms for emissions trading and project-based clean development. Although the Kyoto Protocol faced challenges in its implementation and effectiveness, it represented an important step towards global climate action.

3.3. Paris Agreement

The Paris Agreement, adopted in 2015, marked a significant milestone in global efforts to combat climate change. It aims to limit global warming to well below 2 degrees Celsius above pre-industrial levels and pursue efforts to limit the temperature increase to 1.5 degrees Celsius. The agreement emphasizes nationally determined contributions (NDCs) through which each country outlines its specific climate actions and targets. It also promotes transparency, adaptation, finance, and technology transfer to support developing nations in their climate efforts. The Paris Agreement has been ratified by the majority of countries, demonstrating global commitment to addressing climate change.

Benefits of Environmental Multilateralism

4.1. Coordinated Global Action

Environmental multilateralism provides a platform for countries to come together and coordinate their efforts to combat climate change. Through negotiations and agreements, nations can align their policies, share best practices, and develop innovative solutions. Multilateralism enables the pooling of resources, expertise, and technologies to achieve collective goals, fostering a global response to climate change that is more effective than individual actions.

4.2. Enhanced Ambition and Commitment

Multilateral processes provide a space for countries to increase their ambition in tackling climate change. By engaging in negotiations, nations can be influenced by the actions and commitments of others, leading to a ripple effect of increased ambition. Multilateral agreements set the stage for regular reviews and updates of countries' climate actions, ensuring that efforts are continually strengthened over time.

4.3. Equitable Burden Sharing

One of the key principles of environmental multilateralism is the principle of common but differentiated responsibilities. This principle recognizes that countries have different historical responsibilities and capacities to address climate change. Multilateral frameworks allow for the fair allocation of responsibilities, taking into account the varying circumstances and capacities of different nations. This ensures that the burden of climate action is shared equitably, promoting global solidarity and cooperation.

4.4. Financial and Technological Support

Environmental multilateralism plays a crucial role in facilitating financial and technological support for developing countries. Multilateral agreements often include provisions for climate finance, where developed countries commit to providing financial resources to support climate mitigation and adaptation efforts in developing nations. Additionally, technology transfer mechanisms are established to facilitate the sharing of clean and sustainable technologies, enabling developing countries to leapfrog to low-carbon development pathways.

Challenges and Criticisms

5.1. Political Will and National Interests

One of the primary challenges of environmental multilateralism is the need to navigate conflicting national interests and political dynamics. Countries may prioritize their short-term economic interests over long-term climate goals, leading to resistance or reluctance to commit to ambitious climate actions. Negotiations can be complex and protracted, requiring compromises and consensus-building among diverse nations with different priorities and agendas.

5.2. Implementation Gap

While multilateral agreements provide a framework for action, the implementation of commitments remains a significant challenge. Countries may struggle to translate their pledges into concrete policies and measures at the national level. Monitoring and accountability mechanisms are crucial to ensure that countries follow through on their commitments and take effective action. Close coordination and support between international institutions and national governments are necessary to bridge the implementation gap.

5.3. Lack of Ambition and Urgency

Critics argue that multilateral efforts to address climate change have been insufficient in terms of ambition and urgency. The targets set under international agreements, such as the Paris Agreement, may fall short of the level of action required to limit global warming to safe levels. The slow pace of negotiations and the time taken to reach consensus on critical issues may hinder the ability to respond effectively to the rapidly escalating climate crisis.

The Way Forward

6.1. Strengthening International Cooperation

In the face of climate change, it is essential to strengthen international cooperation and bolster the effectiveness of environmental multilateralism. Countries need to enhance their commitments and actions, raising ambition in line with the urgency of the climate crisis. This requires building trust among nations, fostering dialogue, and facilitating the exchange of knowledge and experiences to encourage collaboration and joint problem-solving.

6.2. Advancing Climate Finance and Technology Transfer

Climate finance and technology transfer mechanisms must be further developed and adequately funded to support developing countries in their climate efforts. Developed countries should fulfill their commitments to provide financial resources and promote technology sharing to ensure a just and equitable transition to a low-carbon economy. Innovative financing models, public-private partnerships, and capacity-building initiatives can enhance the effectiveness of climate finance and technology transfer.

6.3. Enhancing Transparency and Accountability

Transparency and accountability are crucial for the success of environmental multilateralism. Regular reporting and review mechanisms should be strengthened to ensure that countries adhere to their commitments and take effective climate actions. Clear guidelines for monitoring, reporting, and verification of emissions and progress towards climate goals are necessary to foster trust and enable comparisons among nations. Civil society engagement and public participation can also contribute to accountability and ensure that the voices of all stakeholders are heard.

6.4. Promoting Climate Diplomacy

Climate diplomacy plays a vital role in fostering cooperation and mobilizing global action on climate change. Diplomatic efforts should focus on building alliances, bridging differences, and finding common ground among countries with diverse interests. Climate diplomats can work towards consensus-building, mediate disputes, and advocate for ambitious climate policies on the international stage. Climate change should be a priority on diplomatic agendas, and partnerships across sectors and stakeholders should be fostered to accelerate progress.

6.5. Mainstreaming Climate Action

To address climate change comprehensively, climate action should be integrated into all sectors and levels of governance. Governments, businesses, civil society organizations, and individuals must work together to mainstream climate considerations into policies, strategies, and everyday practices. This includes promoting sustainable energy systems, transitioning to low-carbon industries, investing in resilient infrastructure, and promoting sustainable consumption and lifestyle choices. Education and awareness campaigns can also play a significant role in fostering a culture of sustainability and climate consciousness.

Climate change poses an unprecedented threat to the environment and human well-being, demanding urgent and collaborative action.

Environmental multilateralism provides a framework for nations to come together, negotiate agreements, and coordinate efforts to address climate change collectively. Through international cooperation, countries can enhance ambition, share resources, and promote equitable burden sharing. However, challenges such as conflicting national interests, implementation gaps, and the need for greater ambition remain. To move forward, it is crucial to strengthen international cooperation, advance climate finance and technology transfer, enhance transparency and accountability, promote climate diplomacy, and mainstream climate action. Only through effective environmental multilateralism can we hope to mitigate the impacts of climate change, protect the environment, and secure a sustainable future for generations to come.

China's Environmental Challenges: A Path to Sustainable Development

China, the world's most populous country and the second-largest economy, has experienced rapid industrialization and urbanization over the past few decades. While this growth has propelled China to global prominence, it has also given rise to significant environmental challenges that threaten the country's sustainable development and the well-being of its people. From air pollution and water scarcity to deforestation and habitat degradation, China faces a complex web of environmental issues that require urgent attention and innovative solutions.

This essay aims to provide a comprehensive introduction to China's environmental challenges, examining the causes, consequences, and potential strategies for addressing these issues. By delving into the country's environmental history, current state, and future prospects, we can gain valuable insights into the complex interplay between economic development, environmental degradation, and the quest for sustainability.

To understand China's environmental challenges, it is essential to examine the historical context in which they have emerged. China's environmental problems have deep roots, stemming from decades of rapid industrialization, urbanization, and agricultural expansion. The country's emphasis on economic growth and lifting its people out of poverty has come at a significant cost to its natural resources and ecosystems.

The Maoist era (1949-1976) witnessed policies that promoted heavy industrialization, collective farming, and large-scale infrastructure development. These measures, though aimed at achieving economic self-sufficiency, often neglected environmental considerations, leading to widespread pollution and ecological degradation.

Key Environmental Challenges:

a. Air Pollution: China's air quality has become a pressing concern, with cities frequently enveloped in smog. The combustion of coal, industrial emissions, vehicle exhaust, and construction activities contribute to high levels of particulate matter, sulfur dioxide, and nitrogen oxides, which have severe implications for public health and quality of life.

b. Water Scarcity: Rapid economic growth, population growth, and climate change have strained China's water resources. Water scarcity is particularly acute in northern China, where agriculture, industry, and urban centers compete for limited freshwater supplies. Pollution from industrial and agricultural sources has further degraded water quality, exacerbating the water scarcity issue.

c. Deforestation and Land Degradation: China has experienced significant deforestation due to urban expansion, infrastructure development, and the demand for timber and agricultural land. Loss of forest cover has led to soil erosion, desertification, and a decline in biodiversity, posing ecological and economic risks.

d. Biodiversity Loss and Habitat Destruction: China is one of the world's biodiversity hotspots, but its diverse ecosystems are under threat. Habitat destruction, poaching, invasive species, and pollution have resulted in the decline and extinction of numerous plant and animal species, disrupting ecosystem functioning and ecological balance.

e. Climate Change: As the world's largest emitter of greenhouse gases, China plays a pivotal role in addressing global climate change. Rising temperatures, changing precipitation patterns, and extreme weather events pose significant challenges to China's agriculture, water resources, and vulnerable populations.

Consequences and Implications:

China's environmental challenges have far-reaching consequences for its population, economy, and global implications. Poor air quality contributes to respiratory diseases and other health problems, resulting in increased healthcare costs and reduced labor productivity. Water scarcity hampers agricultural production and industrial operations, affecting food security and economic growth. Deforestation and habitat destruction undermine ecosystem services and the country's ecological balance, jeopardizing long-term sustainability. Moreover, climate change impacts amplify existing environmental challenges and pose new risks to China's economic and social stability.

Government Initiatives and Policies:

Recognizing the urgency of addressing environmental challenges, the Chinese government has taken significant steps to promote sustainable development. The government's Five-Year Plans have increasingly incorporated environmental targets and initiatives to reduce pollution and promote green growth. China has implemented various policies and regulations to curb air pollution, enhance water resource management, restore degraded lands, protect endangered species, and mitigate climate change. The government has also invested heavily in renewable energy sources such as wind, solar, and hydropower, aiming to reduce the country's reliance on fossil fuels and improve air quality.

Additionally, China has demonstrated global leadership in environmental initiatives, such as the Paris Agreement on climate change. The country has committed to peaking its carbon emissions by 2030 and achieving carbon neutrality by 2060. These ambitious targets signal China's determination to transition towards a low-carbon economy and contribute to global efforts in mitigating climate change.

Challenges and Opportunities:

While China's efforts in addressing environmental challenges are commendable, several obstacles must be overcome to achieve sustainable development. Balancing economic growth with environmental protection remains a delicate task, as the country grapples with the need to provide employment, improve living standards, and alleviate poverty. The sheer scale and complexity of China's environmental issues require comprehensive and integrated approaches that consider social, economic, and environmental dimensions.

Furthermore, effective implementation and enforcement of environmental policies at the local level are crucial. Local governments and industries often face challenges in aligning their interests and practices with national environmental targets. Improving environmental governance, enhancing transparency, and strengthening environmental law enforcement are essential for achieving desired outcomes.

Despite these challenges, China also possesses immense opportunities to address its environmental issues. The government's focus on innovation and technological advancement can play a pivotal role in developing clean energy solutions, improving industrial efficiency, and implementing sustainable urban planning. Harnessing the potential of emerging technologies, such as artificial intelligence and big data, can facilitate smarter environmental management and decision-making.

Moreover, China's large consumer market provides opportunities for sustainable consumption and production patterns. By promoting eco friendly products, green manufacturing practices, and consumer awareness, China can foster a culture of sustainability and drive market demand for environmentally friendly alternatives.

International Collaboration and Cooperation:

China's environmental challenges transcend national boundaries, necessitating international collaboration and cooperation. The interconnectedness of global ecosystems and the shared responsibility to address climate change demand collective action. International cooperation can facilitate knowledge sharing, technology transfer, and capacity building, enabling China to benefit from global expertise and best practices.

China's Belt and Road Initiative (BRI), a massive infrastructure development project spanning multiple countries, presents both challenges and opportunities in terms of environmental sustainability. Collaborative efforts between China and partner countries can ensure that BRI projects incorporate environmental considerations, promote green technology transfer, and adhere to sustainable development principles.

China's environmental challenges are multifaceted and complex, posing significant risks to the country's sustainable development and the well-being of its people. However, with concerted efforts, innovative solutions, and strong political will, China has the potential to address these challenges and transition towards a more sustainable future. The government's commitment to environmental protection, coupled with international collaboration, can facilitate the implementation of effective policies, technological advancements, and behavioral changes necessary to mitigate environmental degradation and promote sustainable development.

By tackling air pollution, water scarcity, deforestation, biodiversity loss, and climate change, China can not only protect its natural resources and ecosystems but also enhance public health, improve living standards, and build a resilient economy. The path to sustainable development requires a balanced approach that integrates economic growth, environmental protection, and social well-being. Only through such an approach can China secure a prosperous and sustainable future for its citizens while contributing to global efforts in addressing the planet's environmental challenges.

China's Climate Change Policies: An Ambitious Path towards Environmental Leadership

Climate change has emerged as one of the most critical global challenges of our time, posing threats to ecosystems, economies, and human well-being. As the world's largest emitter of greenhouse gases (GHGs), China plays a pivotal role in shaping the future of our planet's climate. Over the past few decades, China has experienced unprecedented economic growth, leading to a significant increase in energy consumption and carbon emissions. However, recognizing the urgent need to address climate change, China has embarked on a transformative journey to become a global leader in mitigating greenhouse gas emissions and fostering sustainable development.

This introduction aims to provide an in-depth analysis of China's climate change policies, examining the key drivers, initiatives, and challenges encountered along its path to combatting climate change. It will explore the factors that have shaped China's approach, the notable policy measures implemented, and the implications of these policies on both domestic and international fronts. Additionally, it will highlight the progress made by China and evaluate the effectiveness of its climate change policies, while also shedding light on the challenges that lie ahead.

Context and Motivation:

1.1 Background:

China's rapid industrialization and economic growth have brought immense prosperity to the nation, but they have also resulted in severe environmental challenges. The environmental consequences, coupled with growing concerns over climate change, have propelled the Chinese government to prioritize sustainable development and adopt comprehensive climate change policies.

1.2 Drivers for Climate Action:

China's climate change policies are motivated by a combination of factors, including the need to address severe air pollution, safeguard public health, ensure energy security, and enhance international standing. The adverse impacts of climate change, such as extreme weather events, sea-level rise, and ecosystem degradation, have also influenced China's commitment to mitigating GHG emissions.

Policy Framework:

2.1 International Commitments:

China's climate change policies are intricately linked to its international commitments. As a signatory to the United Nations Framework Convention on Climate Change (UNFCCC), China has actively participated in global climate negotiations and ratified the Paris Agreement. China's commitments under the Paris Agreement include peak carbon dioxide emissions by 2030 and achieving carbon neutrality by 2060.

2.2 National Policy Measures:

China has implemented a range of policy measures at the national level to drive its climate change agenda. These include establishing emission reduction targets, promoting renewable energy sources, enhancing energy efficiency, implementing carbon pricing mechanisms, and adopting low carbon transportation systems. The Chinese government has also introduced regulatory frameworks and financial incentives to support the transition to a low-carbon economy.

Key Policy Initiatives:

3.1 Renewable Energy Expansion:

China has become a global leader in renewable energy deployment. It has made substantial investments in wind, solar, hydro, and nuclear power, leading to significant capacity additions. China's efforts to scale up renewable energy have not only contributed to reducing carbon emissions but have also stimulated technological advancements, cost reductions, and job creation in the clean energy sector.

3.2 Energy Efficiency Measures:

Recognizing the importance of energy efficiency in reducing carbon emissions, China has implemented rigorous energy-saving programs. These programs focus on improving industrial processes, enhancing building efficiency standards, and promoting the use of energy-efficient appliances. Energy efficiency targets have been set for various sectors, encouraging companies to adopt cleaner technologies and practices.

3.3 Carbon Market Initiatives:

China launched the world's largest carbon market in 2021, known as the national emissions trading scheme (ETS). The ETS covers key industries and aims to cap and reduce carbon emissions. By creating a market-based mechanism, China seeks to incentivize emission reductions, encourage low-carbon innovation, and drive the transition to a low-carbon economy.

Progress and Achievements:

China's climate change policies have yielded significant progress and achievements in various aspects of emission reduction and sustainable development.

4.1 Emission Reduction:

China has made substantial strides in reducing its carbon emissions. It has successfully decoupled its economic growth from carbon intensity, with the carbon intensity of its GDP decreasing by over 48% from 2005 to 2020. China's efforts have resulted in the closure of outdated and inefficient coal-fired power plants, the promotion of cleaner energy sources, and the implementation of stringent emission standards for industries.

4.2 Renewable Energy Deployment:

China has become a global leader in renewable energy capacity, particularly in wind and solar power. It has achieved remarkable growth in installed renewable energy capacity, accounting for a significant share of the world's total renewable energy capacity. China's investments in clean energy infrastructure have not only reduced reliance on fossil fuels but have also spurred innovation and technological advancements in the renewable energy sector.

4.3 Electric Vehicle Adoption:

China has taken significant steps to promote the adoption of electric vehicles (EVs) as a means to reduce transportation emissions. It has implemented supportive policies, such as financial incentives, subsidies, and charging infrastructure development, leading to a rapid increase in EV sales. China is now the largest market for EVs, contributing to a significant reduction in carbon emissions from the transportation sector.

4.4 International Cooperation:

China has actively engaged in international cooperation on climate change, forging partnerships and collaborations with other countries and international organizations. It has provided financial and technical assistance to developing countries to support their climate change mitigation and adaptation efforts. China's involvement in global initiatives, such as the Belt and Road Initiative, has also incorporated sustainability principles, including promoting clean energy and green infrastructure development.

Challenges and Future Outlook:

While China has made commendable progress in its climate change policies, several challenges and areas of improvement remain.

5.1 Coal Dependency:

China's reliance on coal as a primary source of energy poses a significant challenge in achieving its emission reduction targets. Despite efforts to reduce coal consumption and promote clean energy alternatives, the sheer size of China's coal industry and its role in supporting economic growth make the transition away from coal complex. Addressing this challenge requires a comprehensive strategy that includes diversifying the energy mix, improving energy efficiency, and implementing stricter environmental regulations.

5.2 Regional Disparities:

China's climate change policies need to address regional disparities in economic development, energy consumption, and emissions. The country's eastern coastal regions have made more progress in reducing emissions compared to the western and central regions, where heavy industries and resource-intensive sectors are concentrated. Ensuring equitable implementation of climate policies across different regions and addressing the unique challenges faced by each region will be crucial for achieving national emission reduction goals.

5.3 Monitoring and Enforcement:

Effective monitoring and enforcement mechanisms are essential for ensuring the implementation and compliance of climate change policies. China needs to strengthen its monitoring systems, enhance transparency, and improve data quality and reporting. Additionally, the enforcement of environmental regulations, particularly in industries with a high carbon footprint, needs to be strengthened to ensure that emission reduction targets are met.

5.4 Just Transition:

As China transitions towards a low-carbon economy, it is essential to consider the social and economic impacts on workers and communities reliant on high-carbon industries. A just transition approach, which prioritizes job creation, skills development, and social protection for affected workers and communities, is crucial to ensure a smooth and inclusive transition.

China's climate change policies reflect a strong commitment to address the challenges posed by climate change and transition towards a sustainable and low-carbon future. The country's ambitious targets, comprehensive policy framework, and significant investments in renewable energy and emission reduction initiatives have resulted in substantial progress and achievements. China's leadership in renewable energy deployment,international cooperation, and the establishment of the national emissions trading scheme demonstrate its determination to become a global leader in combating climate change.

However, China still faces significant challenges, including its heavy reliance on coal, regional disparities in development, and the need for improved monitoring and enforcement mechanisms. Overcoming these challenges will require sustained efforts and continued innovation in policy implementation.

Looking ahead, China's climate change policies will play a crucial role in shaping global climate action. As the world's largest emitter and a major economic power, China's commitment to sustainability and emission reduction will influence the trajectory of global efforts to combat climate change. China's leadership in renewable energy development and low-carbon technologies has the potential to drive global innovation and accelerate the transition to a green economy.

Furthermore, China's involvement in international cooperation and its role in initiatives like the Belt and Road Initiative can contribute to promoting sustainable development practices globally. By sharing its experiences, knowledge, and resources, China can help developing countries in their climate change mitigation and adaptation efforts.

In conclusion, China's climate change policies represent a bold and ambitious path towards environmental leadership. The country has recognized the urgent need to address climate change and has taken significant steps to reduce carbon emissions, promote renewable energy, and drive sustainable development. While challenges remain, China's progress in emission reduction, renewable energy deployment, and international cooperation underscores its commitment to tackling climate change. As the world continues to grapple with the climate crisis, China's climate change policies will undoubtedly play a crucial role in shaping a more sustainable and resilient future for the planet.

China's Role in International Climate Negotiations: A Driving Force for Global Environmental Action

Climate change is an urgent global challenge that requires concerted efforts and cooperation from all nations. As the world's largest emitter of greenhouse gases (GHGs), China holds a critical role in addressing this pressing issue. China's journey in international climate negotiations has witnessed significant transformations, from being seen as a barrier to progress to emerging as a key player and driving force for global environmental action. This essay aims to explore China's evolving role in international climate negotiations, analyzing its historical context, policy developments, and the implications of its actions on global climate governance.

Historical Context

China's historical context provides insights into its changing role in international climate negotiations.

As an emerging economy and developing nation, China's primary focus for decades was rapid industrialization and poverty alleviation. This pursuit of economic growth resulted in substantial GHG emissions, making China the largest contributor to global carbon dioxide emissions since 2005. Consequently, China's stance in international climate negotiations was often characterized by concerns over sovereignty, development rights, and the principle of common but differentiated responsibilities (CBDR).

Policy Developments

Despite initial reservations, China gradually recognized the need to address climate change and started adopting policies and measures to mitigate its carbon footprint. The following policy developments highlight China's growing commitment to addressing climate change:

2.1. Renewable Energy Expansion

China has become a global leader in renewable energy deployment. The country has made substantial investments in wind, solar, hydro, and nuclear energy, driving down the cost of renewable technologies and enabling significant capacity additions. China's renewable energy capacity has surpassed that of any other country, positioning it as a crucial player in the global energy transition.

2.2. Emissions Reduction Targets

Recognizing the urgency of climate action, China has set ambitious emissions reduction targets. In 2009, China pledged to reduce its carbon intensity (CO_2 emissions per unit of GDP) by 40-45% from 2005 levels by 2020. Furthermore, in 2015, China committed to peaking its carbon dioxide emissions by 2030 and increasing the share of non-fossil fuels in its primary energy consumption to around 20%. These targets represent significant steps towards decoupling economic growth from carbon emissions.

China has launched the world's largest carbon market, covering multiple sectors and involving thousands of companies. The establishment of the national carbon market demonstrates China's commitment to market-based mechanisms for emissions reduction. It also provides an opportunity to explore potential collaborations and knowledge sharing in carbon pricing with other nations.

Implications for Global Climate Governance

3.1. Shifting the Global Narrative

China's transition from a passive participant to an active contributor in climate negotiations has shifted the global narrative on climate action. By embracing renewable energy, setting ambitious targets, and adopting market-based mechanisms,

China has demonstrated that sustainable development and economic growth can go hand in hand. This shift has not only inspired other developing nations but has also pressured developed countries to enhance their climate commitments.

3.2. Collaboration and South-South Cooperation

China's involvement in international climate negotiations has fostered collaboration and South-South cooperation. Through initiatives like the Belt and Road Initiative (BRI), China has been investing in renewable energy projects in developing countries, contributing to their sustainable development and reducing their reliance on fossil fuels. This approach not only supports global emissions reduction efforts but also strengthens China's position as a leader in climate diplomacy.

3.3. Technology and Innovation

China's rapid advancements in renewable energy technologies and its domestic market scale have positioned it as a hub for green technology and innovation. China's investments in research and development have resulted in breakthroughs in areas such as solar power, electric vehicles, and energy storage. These advancements have global implications, as they contribute to the availability and affordability of clean technologies worldwide. China's willingness to share its technological expertise and collaborate with other countries in research and development initiatives promotes global innovation in the fight against climate change.

3.4. Multilateral Diplomacy

China's engagement in multilateral forums such as the United Nations Framework Convention on Climate Change (UNFCCC) and the Conference of the Parties (COP) has been instrumental in shaping global climate governance. As a major player in international climate negotiations, China has the capacity to influence the outcomes of these forums, contributing to the development of international agreements, such as the Paris Agreement. China's active participation and constructive diplomacy contribute to the collective effort in addressing climate change at the global level.

Challenges and Areas for Improvement

4.1. Transitioning from Coal

China's heavy reliance on coal for energy production remains a significant challenge. Despite efforts to promote renewable energy, coal continues to dominate China's energy mix, contributing to high levels of air pollution and greenhouse gas emissions. Accelerating the transition away from coal and towards cleaner energy sources is crucial for China to achieve its emissions reduction targets and demonstrate global climate leadership.

4.2. Monitoring and Transparency

Ensuring accurate monitoring, reporting, and verification of emissions is essential for effective climate governance. China's large size and complex industrial landscape make it challenging to monitor and track emissions accurately. Enhancing transparency and data quality will boost international confidence in China's climate commitments and facilitate greater trust among nations.

4.3. International Cooperation

Strengthening international cooperation is vital to address global climate challenges effectively. While China has engaged in bilateral and multilateral partnerships, there is room for further collaboration with other nations. Enhancing information sharing, technology transfer, and capacity building initiatives can foster greater global solidarity in tackling climate change.

4.4. Addressing Adaptation and Climate Justice

As a developing nation, China faces significant challenges in adapting to the impacts of climate change. Rising sea levels, extreme weather events, and water scarcity are some of the issues that require attention. China can play a crucial role in advocating for adaptation measures and climate justice, ensuring that vulnerable communities receive the support they need to cope with and recover from climate-related impacts.

China's role in international climate negotiations has undergone a remarkable transformation, positioning the nation as a driving force for global environmental action. Through policy developments, renewable energy expansion, emissions reduction targets, and multilateral engagement, China has demonstrated a growing commitment to addressing climate change. Its evolving role has shifted the global narrative, fostered collaboration, promoted technology and innovation, and strengthened multilateral climate governance.

However, challenges remain, and China must continue its efforts to transition away from coal, enhance transparency, strengthen international cooperation, and address adaptation and climate justice. By addressing these challenges, China can further solidify its position as a global leader in climate action, inspiring other nations and driving the collective effort to mitigate climate change.

As the world grapples with the urgency of climate change, China's role in international climate negotiations will continue to evolve and shape the future of global climate governance. The collaboration and collective action of all nations, with China playing a pivotal role, are essential to effectively combat this global challenge and secure a sustainable and prosperous future for generations to come.

Part IV: Challenges and Opportunities

In an increasingly interconnected and interdependent world, multilateralism has emerged as a critical framework for addressing global challenges and promoting cooperation among nations. Multilateralism refers to the practice of multiple countries coming together to collectively address common concerns, negotiate agreements, and make joint decisions on global issues. It encompasses a wide range of fields, including politics, economics, trade, security, and the environment. As one of the world's most populous and influential countries, China's engagement with multilateralism is of utmost importance. This paper explores the challenges and opportunities that China faces in its pursuit of multilateralism.

China's rise as a global power over the past few decades has significantly transformed the dynamics of the international system. With its remarkable economic growth, expanding military capabilities, and growing influence, China has become a key player in shaping the multilateral order. However, its ascent has also posed challenges to the existing global order, leading to debates and uncertainties about China's intentions and the implications of its rise for the future of multilateralism.

One of the key challenges that China faces in multilateralism is striking a balance between its domestic interests and its international obligations. As an emerging economy, China's primary focus has been on economic development and poverty alleviation within its borders. This has sometimes led to tensions between China's pursuit of national interests and its commitments to multilateral institutions. For example, China's economic policies, such as its state-led industrialization and trade practices, have been a subject of contention among other countries, particularly in the context of the World Trade Organization (WTO). China's adherence to international trade norms and its willingness to level the playing field for other countries have been questioned, raising concerns about the fairness and inclusivity of multilateral trade.

Another challenge for China in multilateralism is navigating its complex relationships with other major powers. The rise of China has inevitably resulted in a shift in global power dynamics, with potential implications for the existing multilateral order. China's relations with the United States, the European Union, and other major powers are characterized by a mixture of cooperation, competition, and strategic rivalry. The intensification of geopolitical tensions, such as the trade war between China and the United States, has strained multilateral institutions and impeded cooperation on shared global challenges. China's ability to effectively engage with other major powers in multilateral forums is crucial for advancing its own interests and contributing to global governance.

Moreover, China's commitment to universal values, human rights, and democratic norms has been a subject of scrutiny in multilateralism. The Chinese government's approach to governance, human rights, and freedom of expression differs significantly from the Western liberal democratic model. This has led to concerns about China's influence on global norms and the potential erosion of human rights standards within multilateral institutions. China's increasing assertiveness in promoting its own vision of governance and development, as exemplified by initiatives such as the Belt and Road Initiative (BRI), has raised questions about the compatibility of China's approach with the principles of inclusivity, transparency, and accountability that underpin multilateralism.

Despite these challenges, China also presents significant opportunities for multilateralism. China's economic prowess and its investments in infrastructure development have the potential to contribute to global economic growth and development. The BRI, for instance, aims to enhance connectivity and promote economic integration across regions, offering opportunities for infrastructure development, trade facilitation, and poverty reduction. China's participation in multilateral institutions such as the Asian Infrastructure Investment Bank (AIIB) and its involvement in global climate change initiatives demonstrate its willingness to contribute to addressing pressing global challenges.

Moreover, China's active engagement with multilateralism can help shape the future of international norms and institutions. As a rising power, China has sought to play a more prominent role in global governance, advocating for a reformed and inclusive multilateral order that better reflects the realities of the 21st century. China has called for greater representation of developing countries in international institutions and has proposed alternative approaches to global governance, such as the concept of "community of common destiny" and "major-country diplomacy with Chinese characteristics." These initiatives indicate China's aspirations to contribute to the evolution of multilateralism in a way that accommodates its interests and those of other developing nations.

Furthermore, China's active participation in multilateral forums provides an opportunity for dialogue, cooperation, and the resolution of global challenges. China has increasingly taken on a leadership role in areas such as climate change, global health, and sustainable development. For instance, China's commitment to the Paris Agreement and its efforts to reduce carbon emissions demonstrate its willingness to work with other countries to tackle climate change. Similarly, China's involvement in international health organizations, such as the World Health Organization (WHO), has allowed for collaborative responses to global health crises, as seen during the COVID-19 pandemic.

China's rise in multilateralism also presents opportunities for enhanced regional integration and cooperation. China's economic influence in Asia has spurred the development of regional initiatives such as the Regional Comprehensive Economic Partnership (RCEP), which encompasses 15 Asia-Pacific countries and aims to promote trade liberalization and economic integration. These regional initiatives have the potential to foster greater cooperation and stability in the region, strengthening multilateralism at both regional and global levels.

In addition, China's emphasis on connectivity and digital technologies can contribute to the advancement of multilateralism in the digital age. China's advancements in areas such as e-commerce, 5G technology, and artificial intelligence present opportunities for innovation and collaboration in multilateral frameworks. However, it is important to ensure that these technologies are harnessed in a manner that respects privacy, security, and human rights, in line with multilateral norms and standards.

To effectively address the challenges and opportunities in multilateralism, China needs to adopt a strategic and principled approach. First and foremost, China should strive to balance its domestic interests with its international commitments. This requires ensuring that its economic policies are aligned with multilateral trade rules, promoting fair competition and a level playing field for all countries. China can also enhance transparency and engagement by actively participating in multilateral negotiations and consultations, seeking input and feedback from other nations. By demonstrating a genuine commitment to inclusivity and cooperation, China can build trust and credibility in multilateral forums.

Second, China should actively engage with other major powers in order to manage geopolitical tensions and foster cooperation. This entails seeking common ground and shared interests, even amid disagreements, and exploring avenues for collaboration on pressing global challenges. China can leverage its economic influence and diplomatic channels to promote dialogue, mediation, and conflict resolution within multilateral institutions.

Third, China should continue to engage in dialogue and exchange with other countries on issues of governance, human rights, and democratic norms. This includes addressing concerns about human rights violations, ensuring freedom of expression and information, and promoting transparency and accountability. China can demonstrate its commitment to multilateral values by actively participating in discussions and initiatives related to human rights and governance, while also respecting the diversity of cultural and political systems across the globe.

Lastly, China should seize the opportunities presented by its economic power, regional influence, and technological advancements to contribute positively to multilateralism. This involves leveraging its economic resources to support sustainable development initiatives, promoting regional integration and cooperation, and fostering innovation and digital connectivity within multilateral frameworks. China can also contribute to the reform and strengthening of existing multilateral institutions, advocating for greater representation and inclusivity.

In conclusion, China's engagement with multilateralism is marked by both challenges and opportunities. As a rising global power, China's actions and policies significantly impact the future trajectory of multilateralism. Striking a balance between its domestic interests and international obligations, navigating complex relationships with other major powers, addressing concerns about universal values and human rights, and leveraging its economic and technological capabilities are crucial for China to effectively contribute to and shape the future of multilateralism.

China's active participation in multilateral forums, such as the United Nations (UN), World Trade Organization (WTO), and regional organizations like the Association of Southeast Asian Nations (ASEAN), provides a platform for dialogue, cooperation, and negotiation on global issues. By actively engaging in these forums, China can demonstrate its willingness to collaborate with other nations and work towards shared solutions. It is through multilateralism that China can address common challenges like climate change, sustainable development, poverty alleviation, and global health crises in a collective and coordinated manner.

Furthermore, China's efforts to promote regional integration through initiatives like the Belt and Road Initiative (BRI) and regional trade agreements like the RCEP have the potential to strengthen multilateralism at both regional and global levels. These initiatives can foster economic cooperation, infrastructure development, and people-to-people exchanges, enhancing connectivity and cooperation among countries.

China's engagement with multilateralism also provides an opportunity to shape the future of international norms and institutions. As a major global player, China's perspectives and proposals can influence the direction and functioning of multilateral institutions. By actively participating in discussions on global governance, China can contribute to the evolution of multilateralism and advocate for reforms that address the changing dynamics of the international system.

However, for China to effectively navigate the challenges and seize the opportunities in multilateralism, it must also address concerns raised by the international community. One key concern is transparency and accountability. China should ensure transparency in its policies, actions, and investments, particularly with regards to initiatives like the BRI. Transparency helps build trust among nations and ensures that projects and partnerships are undertaken in a sustainable and inclusive manner.

Another concern is the protection of human rights and the promotion of democratic norms. China's approach to governance and human rights has been a subject of criticism and scrutiny by the international community. To effectively engage in multilateralism, China should address these concerns and work towards the protection of human rights, freedom of expression, and the rule of law. By upholding these universal values, China can strengthen its position as a responsible global actor and contribute to the development of a more just and equitable multilateral order.

China's engagement with multilateralism also requires a proactive approach to manage potential conflicts and foster cooperation with other major powers, particularly the United States. The ongoing geopolitical tensions between China and the U.S., as well as other major powers, have strained multilateral institutions and hindered progress on global challenges. By actively seeking common ground, de-escalating tensions, and exploring opportunities for collaboration, China can contribute to a more stable and cooperative multilateral environment.

In conclusion, China's challenges and opportunities in multilateralism are intertwined and complex. While China's rise as a global power has presented challenges to the existing multilateral order, it also offers significant opportunities for collaborative solutions and inclusive global governance. By balancing its domestic interests with international obligations, engaging with other major powers, addressing concerns about human rights and democratic norms, and leveraging its economic and technological capabilities, China can effectively contribute to the advancement of multilateralism. Through active participation, dialogue, and cooperation, China can shape the future of multilateralism and promote a more inclusive, sustainable, and prosperous world order.

Balancing National Interests and Global Responsibilities

In an increasingly interconnected and interdependent world, the balancing act between national interests and global responsibilities has become a crucial challenge for nations. National interests encompass a country's economic, security, and political priorities, while global responsibilities refer to the collective efforts required to address global challenges and promote global well-being.

Striking a balance between these two dimensions is essential for sustainable development, peaceful coexistence, and effective global governance. This paper delves into the complexities, dilemmas, and strategies involved in balancing national interests and global responsibilities.

The Complexity of Balancing National Interests and Global Responsibilities

National interests are shaped by a country's history, culture, geography, and socioeconomic conditions. Governments are accountable to their citizens, and their primary focus is often on promoting their nation's welfare and security. Economic prosperity, territorial integrity, and political stability are fundamental objectives that governments strive to achieve. However, in an interconnected world, national interests cannot be pursued in isolation. Global challenges such as climate change, pandemics, terrorism, and economic interdependencies require collective action and shared responsibilities.

The complexity arises from the fact that national interests and global responsibilities are not always aligned. There are instances where pursuing national interests may conflict with global objectives. For example, a country heavily reliant on fossil fuel exports may resist efforts to reduce carbon emissions, as it could negatively impact its economy and national energy security. Similarly, a country facing internal political challenges may prioritize stability over democratic principles, which can be at odds with global expectations for human rights and good governance.

The Dilemmas in Balancing National Interests and Global Responsibilities

The balancing act between national interests and global responsibilities gives rise to dilemmas that policymakers must navigate. These dilemmas are often characterized by trade-offs, competing priorities, and conflicting demands. Some of the common dilemmas include:

Economic Growth versus Environmental Sustainability: Economic growth is a primary national interest for many countries, as it brings prosperity and improved living standards. However, pursuing economic growth without considering its environmental impact can undermine global efforts to combat climate change and protect the planet's resources.

National Security versus International Cooperation: Ensuring national security is a paramount concern for governments. However, unilateral actions taken solely in pursuit of national security, such as protectionist trade policies or military interventions, can strain international relations and impede global cooperation on shared challenges.

Sovereignty versus Humanitarian Intervention: The principle of sovereignty asserts a country's right to govern its own affairs without external interference. However, instances of human rights abuses, genocide, or humanitarian crises may create a moral imperative for international intervention, even if it infringes on national sovereignty.

Short-term Interests versus Long-term Sustainability: Political leaders often face pressure to deliver short-term results to appease domestic constituents. However, global challenges such as climate change and sustainable development require long-term planning and investments that may not yield immediate benefits but are crucial for future well-being.

Strategies for Balancing National Interests and Global Responsibilities

While the complexities and dilemmas are inherent in balancing national interests and global responsibilities, there are strategies that nations can adopt to navigate this delicate equilibrium. These strategies involve reconciling divergent interests, fostering cooperation, and embracing multilateralism. Some key strategies include:

Multilateral Diplomacy and Cooperation: Engaging in multilateral forums, such as the United Nations, regional organizations, and bilateral agreements, allows countries to find common ground, negotiate compromises, and collectively address global challenges. By fostering a culture of cooperation, nations can reconcile national interests with global responsibilities and work towards mutually beneficial outcomes.

Inclusive and Sustainable Economic Development: Economic development is a vital national interest, but it can be pursued in a way that aligns with global responsibilities. Embracing sustainable practices, promoting inclusive growth, and prioritizing social and environmental considerations in economic policies can ensure that national economic interests are harmonized with global goals, such as poverty reduction, environmental protection, and social equity.

Responsible Global Citizenship: Nations can demonstrate their commitment to global responsibilities by being responsible global citizens. This entails actively participating in international efforts to address global challenges, contributing to development aid and humanitarian assistance, and upholding international norms and standards. By fulfilling their global responsibilities, countries can enhance their credibility and influence in international affairs while safeguarding their national interests.

Constructive Engagement and Dialogue: Constructive engagement and dialogue are essential for reconciling conflicting interests and finding common ground. Diplomatic channels, bilateral negotiations, and dialogue platforms can facilitate understanding, build trust, and create opportunities for mutually beneficial outcomes. By engaging in open and transparent dialogue, nations can bridge differences, seek win-win solutions, and strike a balance between national interests and global responsibilities.

Forward-looking Policy Planning: Governments need to adopt long-term perspectives and consider the implications of their policies on global dynamics. By incorporating global responsibilities into their policy planning processes, countries can anticipate and mitigate potential conflicts between national interests and global goals. This requires a comprehensive understanding of global trends, early identification of emerging challenges, and proactive policy adjustments to ensure compatibility between national and global priorities.

Promoting Norms and Values: Nations can contribute to global responsibilities by promoting and upholding universal norms and values. Respect for human rights, democratic governance, rule of law, and adherence to international agreements and conventions are not only moral imperatives but also facilitate international cooperation and stability. By embodying and advocating for these norms and values, countries can build trust, foster cooperation, and effectively balance their national interests with their global responsibilities.

Innovative Partnerships and Collaborations: Collaborative partnerships with other nations, international organizations, civil society, and the private sector can enhance the capacity of countries to address global challenges while advancing their national interests. Through joint research and development, technology transfer, knowledge sharing, and resource pooling, nations can leverage collective expertise and resources to tackle complex issues that transcend national boundaries.

Balancing national interests and global responsibilities is a complex and nuanced endeavor for nations in today's interconnected world. The pursuit of national interests is essential for ensuring the welfare and security of nations, while global responsibilities require collective action to address shared challenges and promote global well-being. Navigating the dilemmas and complexities of this balancing act requires strategic and forward-thinking approaches.

By embracing multilateralism, fostering cooperation, and engaging in constructive dialogue, countries can reconcile divergent interests and seek mutually beneficial outcomes. Promoting inclusive and sustainable economic development, being responsible global citizens, and upholding universal norms and values are essential for striking a balance between national interests and global responsibilities. Forward-looking policy planning, innovative partnerships, and collaborative approaches can further strengthen the ability of nations to address global challenges while safeguarding their national interests.

In the pursuit of this delicate balance, nations have the opportunity to demonstrate leadership, build trust, and contribute to the advancement of a more equitable, peaceful, and prosperous world order. By recognizing that national interests and global responsibilities are interconnected, countries can move towards a harmonious and mutually beneficial relationship, ultimately fostering a more sustainable and prosperous future for all.

Sovereignty Concerns and National Interests

Sovereignty concerns and national interests play a crucial role in shaping the policies and actions of states in the international arena. Sovereignty refers to the supreme authority of a state to govern its territory, make decisions, and pursue its own interests without external interference. National interests encompass a range of objectives, including security, economic prosperity, territorial integrity, cultural preservation, and the well-being of citizens. This paper explores the significance of sovereignty concerns and national interests in international relations, examining their impact on state behavior and the challenges they pose to multilateralism and global cooperation.

Sovereignty Concerns

Sovereignty is a fundamental principle of the international system, underpinning the independence and autonomy of states. Sovereignty concerns arise when states perceive their authority, territorial integrity, or decision-making capacity to be threatened or undermined by external actors or institutions. These concerns can stem from various factors, including territorial disputes, interference in domestic affairs, or challenges to the legitimacy of the government.

Territorial disputes are a primary source of sovereignty concerns. Conflicts over land, maritime boundaries, or resources can arise between neighboring states, leading to tensions and potential threats to sovereignty. For example, the ongoing disputes in the South China Sea involving multiple countries, including China, Vietnam, and the Philippines, revolve around conflicting territorial claims, which directly impact sovereignty concerns in the region. Similarly, conflicts in regions like Kashmir or Crimea highlight how sovereignty concerns related to territorial integrity can lead to protracted disputes and geopolitical tensions.

Interference in domestic affairs is another significant sovereignty concern. States often resist external attempts to influence their political systems, governance, or internal policies. They view such interference as encroachments on their sovereignty and an infringement on their right to self-determination. This concern is particularly pronounced in cases where external actors support opposition movements, impose sanctions, or engage in covert operations to manipulate domestic political processes. Examples include Russia's annexation of Crimea, where it cited sovereignty concerns to justify its actions, or China's opposition to foreign criticism of its human rights record, framing it as an interference in its internal affairs.

Challenges to the legitimacy of the government can also trigger sovereignty concerns. States consider their domestic governance structures and political systems as legitimate expressions of their sovereignty. Any external pressure or criticism that challenges the legitimacy of the government is often perceived as an attack on their sovereignty. This concern is prevalent in cases where international actors question the democratic processes, human rights records, or governance practices of states. For instance, when the United States or European Union imposes sanctions on countries accused of human rights violations, those countries often view it as an infringement on their sovereignty and a challenge to their legitimacy.

National interests encompass the objectives and priorities of a state, which guide its policies and actions. They are shaped by various factors, including geography, history, culture, ideology, economic considerations, and security concerns. National interests serve as a compass for states to navigate the complexities of international relations and make decisions that advance their goals and protect their core values.

Security is a primary national interest for states. The protection of their territorial integrity, sovereignty, and citizens is paramount. States invest significant resources in maintaining strong military capabilities, forging alliances, and engaging in regional security arrangements to safeguard their security interests. For example, the United States' pursuit of military interventions in Iraq and Afghanistan can be traced back to its national security concerns regarding terrorism and the prevention of attacks on its soil.

Economic prosperity is another crucial national interest. States seek to ensure sustainable economic growth, access to resources, and favorable trading conditions to enhance the well-being of their citizens. This drives states to pursue economic policies that promote domestic industries, attract foreign investment, and foster international trade. For instance, China's emphasis on economic development and its pursuit of initiatives like the Belt and Road Initiative (BRI) exemplify its commitment to advancing its national economic interests through infrastructure development and enhanced trade connectivity.

Cultural preservation and identity also shape national interests. States often prioritize the preservation and promotion of their cultural heritage, language, and traditions. This interest is particularly pronounced in cases where states perceive external influences as a threat to their cultural identity. For example, countries like France and Japan have implemented policies to protect their cultural industries and promote their national languages in the face of globalization and the dominance of English.

Territorial expansion and preservation of influence are historical national interests that continue to shape state behavior. States may seek to expand their territories or assert control over strategic regions to enhance their power and influence. This interest can be observed in historical examples like the scramble for Africa in the late 19th century or contemporary actions such as Russia's annexation of Crimea.

Challenges to Multilateralism and Global Cooperation

While sovereignty concerns and national interests are legitimate considerations for states, they can also present challenges to multilateralism and global cooperation. Multilateralism refers to the practice of multiple countries coming together to collectively address common concerns and make joint decisions on global issues. It relies on the willingness of states to compromise, collaborate, and prioritize collective interests over narrow national interests. However, sovereignty concerns and national interests can sometimes hinder this cooperative spirit and impede effective multilateral action.

Firstly, sovereignty concerns can lead to a reluctance to cede decision-making authority to international institutions or abide by multilateral agreements States may fear that such actions could undermine their sovereignty or compromise their national interests. This reluctance can create barriers to effective multilateral cooperation, especially in areas that require collective action, such as global climate change or arms control agreements. For example, the United States' withdrawal from the Paris Agreement under the Trump administration was driven, in part, by concerns over sovereignty and perceived negative impacts on the U.S. economy.

Secondly, national interests can foster competition and conflicts of interest among states, hindering cooperation in multilateral forums. States may prioritize their own interests over collective action, leading to disagreements, deadlock, and the inability to reach consensus on important global issues. Economic competition, territorial disputes, or ideological differences can exacerbate these conflicts of interest. For instance, the United States and China's competition for economic dominance and geopolitical influence has resulted in trade tensions, technological rivalry, and strategic competition that hinder multilateral cooperation.

Thirdly, divergent views on human rights, governance, and values can create obstacles to multilateral cooperation. States with different political systems and cultural backgrounds may have conflicting perspectives on issues such as freedom of speech, human rights, or democratic governance. These differences can impede the formation of consensus or common approaches within multilateral institutions, limiting their effectiveness in addressing these challenges. The debates surrounding China's human rights practices or Russia's actions in Crimea illustrate how sovereignty concerns and differing interpretations of universal values can hinder multilateral cooperation on human rights issues.

Overcoming Challenges and Promoting Global Cooperation

Addressing sovereignty concerns and reconciling national interests with the principles of multilateralism requires a strategic and inclusive approach. To promote global cooperation, states can undertake several actions:

Constructive dialogue and engagement: States should engage in open and constructive dialogue to understand each other's concerns, perspectives, and interests. This dialogue can help build trust, identify common ground, and explore avenues for compromise and cooperation.

Compromise and flexibility: States need to demonstrate willingness to compromise and be flexible in finding solutions that balance national interests with collective objectives. This requires recognizing the interconnectedness of global challenges and the shared responsibility to address them.

Strengthening multilateral institutions: States should invest in strengthening multilateral institutions, improving their transparency, accountability, and effectiveness. This can enhance the confidence of states in the multilateral system and promote greater participation and commitment to multilateral cooperation.

Respect for sovereignty and diversity: It is crucial to respect the sovereignty of states and their right to make decisions in accordance with their national interests. Multilateral cooperation should be based on the principle of non-interference in internal affairs, while also upholding universal values and human rights.

Finding common interests: States should identify areas of common interest and shared objectives where cooperation can be pursued. By focusing on mutual benefits and common goals, states can overcome sovereignty concerns and work together towards collective solutions.

Diplomatic engagement and conflict resolution: Diplomatic engagement and effective conflict resolution mechanisms are essential for managing disputes and tensions arising from sovereignty concerns. States should prioritize peaceful dialogue and negotiation to address conflicts and find mutually acceptable solutions.

Promoting inclusivity and equitable representation: Multilateral institutions should strive for inclusivity and equitable representation to ensure that the voices and interests of all states, particularly those from the Global South, are adequately represented. This can help address perceptions of power imbalances and foster greater trust in the multilateral system.

Long-term perspective and sustainable solutions: States should adopt a long-term perspective and focus on sustainable solutions that benefit all parties involved. This requires moving beyond short-term interests and considering the long-term consequences of actions and policies.

Sovereignty concerns and national interests are integral to the behavior and decision-making of states in the international arena. While these considerations are legitimate, they can also pose challenges to multilateralism and global cooperation. Overcoming these challenges requires a balanced approach that respects sovereignty, promotes dialogue, and seeks common interests. By finding ways to reconcile national interests with collective objectives, states can foster a more cooperative and effective multilateral system. Ultimately, addressing sovereignty concerns and promoting global cooperation are vital for tackling shared challenges and advancing the collective well-being of states and their citizens in an interconnected world.

Chinese Leadership in Multilateral Institutions

China's rise as a global power has been accompanied by an increasing leadership role in multilateral institutions. As one of the world's largest economies and most populous countries, China's engagement with multilateralism has significant implications for global governance and the shaping of international norms and institutions. This paper explores China's leadership in multilateral institutions, examining its motivations, strategies, and the impact of its leadership on the global order.

Motivations for Chinese Leadership

China's motivations for assuming a leadership role in multilateral institutions can be attributed to both domestic and international factors. Domestically, China seeks to protect and promote its national interests and enhance its international standing. Leadership in multilateral institutions allows China to shape global norms and rules in ways that align with its own interests and preferences. It provides opportunities to influence decision-making processes and ensure that the international system accommodates China's economic, political, and security concerns.

Internationally, China aspires to be recognized as a responsible global power and gain legitimacy in the international community. Leadership in multilateral institutions provides a platform for China to demonstrate its willingness to cooperate, contribute to global challenges, and play a constructive role in addressing shared concerns. By actively engaging in multilateralism, China aims to dispel concerns about its rise and establish itself as a reliable and influential actor in the international arena.

Strategies for Chinese Leadership

China employs various strategies to assert its leadership in multilateral institutions. One key strategy is active participation and engagement. China consistently participates in multilateral forums, such as the United Nations (UN), World Trade Organization (WTO), and the Group of Twenty (G20), among others. Through active engagement, China seeks to shape the agenda, contribute to decision-making processes, and advance its own interests. This involves advocating for policies and initiatives that align with China's priorities and leveraging its diplomatic influence to build alliances and partnerships.

Another strategy is resource mobilization. China's economic clout allows it to provide financial resources and investments to support multilateral initiatives. For instance, China has established the Asian Infrastructure Investment Bank (AIIB) and the Silk Road Fund, which contribute to infrastructure development in Asia and beyond. By providing financial support, China enhances its influence within multilateral institutions and gains the support of other countries that benefit from its investments.

Additionally, China employs a strategy of norm promotion and agenda-setting. Through its active engagement in multilateral forums, China seeks to shape international norms and standards in line with its own values and preferences. This includes advocating for the principles of non-interference in internal affairs and respect for national sovereignty, which resonate with other countries that have similar concerns. China also promotes its own initiatives, such as the Belt and Road Initiative (BRI), as a model for economic development and connectivity. By setting its own agenda, China can influence the priorities and narratives within multilateral institutions.

Impact of Chinese Leadership

China's leadership in multilateral institutions has had a significant impact on the global order. One notable impact is the shift in power dynamics. China's rise as a global power has challenged the traditional dominance of Western powers in multilateral institutions. China's increased influence and assertiveness have led to debates and adjustments in the distribution of power and decision-making processes within these institutions. As a result, multilateral institutions are increasingly reflective of the evolving geopolitical landscape, with China playing a more prominent role in shaping global governance.

China's leadership has also brought changes to the policy priorities and approaches within multilateral institutions. For example, China's emphasis on economic development and poverty alleviation has influenced the focus of international development agendas. China's support for infrastructure development and connectivity, as exemplified by the BRI, has gained attention and influenced discussions on regional and global connectivity initiatives. Moreover, China's approach to trade and investment has challenged the traditional models of economic governance and prompted debates on issues such as market access, intellectual property rights, and fair competition within multilateral trade frameworks.

Furthermore, China's leadership has had implications for global norms and values. China's advocacy for the principles of non-interference and respect for national sovereignty has resonated with some countries that have concerns about external interference. This has led to debates about the universality of human rights and the extent to which global norms should be influenced by diverse cultural and political contexts. China's leadership in multilateral institutions has also sparked discussions about the balance between national interests and collective responsibilities, raising questions about the role of multilateralism in addressing global challenges.

Moreover, China's leadership in multilateral institutions has brought both opportunities and challenges for other countries. On one hand, China's economic resources and investments have provided opportunities for infrastructure development, trade facilitation, and poverty reduction in recipient countries. China's engagement in regional and global initiatives, such as the AIIB and the BRI, has allowed countries to access financing and participate in connectivity projects. On the other hand, concerns have been raised about the terms and conditions of Chinese investments, potential debt burdens, and the impact on local economies and environments. This highlights the need for careful scrutiny and evaluation of the implications of China's leadership in multilateral institutions.

China's leadership in multilateral institutions has also led to debates about the future direction of global governance. Some argue that China's rise challenges the liberal international order and the principles of democratic governance, human rights, and the rule of law that underpin it. They raise concerns about the potential erosion of these values within multilateral institutions and the impact on global norms. Others argue that China's leadership brings diversity and alternative perspectives to the table, enriching the discussions and enabling a more inclusive and multipolar global order.

China's leadership in multilateral institutions is a significant aspect of its rise as a global power. Motivated by domestic and international factors, China actively engages in multilateralism to protect its national interests, enhance its international standing, and shape global governance. Through strategies such as active participation, resource mobilization, norm promotion, and agenda-setting, China asserts its influence within multilateral institutions and contributes to shaping the global order.

The impact of Chinese leadership in multilateral institutions is far-reaching. It has challenged the traditional power dynamics and prompted adjustments in decision-making processes. China's leadership has influenced policy priorities, economic governance, and the balance between national interests and collective responsibilities. It has also sparked debates about global norms, values, and the future direction of global governance.

China's leadership in multilateral institutions presents both opportunities and challenges for other countries. While China's economic resources and investments can contribute to development and connectivity, concerns exist regarding the terms and conditions of Chinese investments and their potential impact on recipient countries. Careful evaluation and scrutiny are essential to ensure that the implications of China's leadership are beneficial and sustainable for all parties involved.

In conclusion, China's leadership in multilateral institutions is a dynamic and evolving phenomenon with significant implications for global governance. As China continues to rise as a global power, its engagement in multilateralism will continue to shape the international order, and the interactions between China and other countries within these institutions will play a crucial role in defining the future of multilateralism.

Managing Geopolitical Tensions in Multilateralism

Managing geopolitical tensions in multilateralism has become increasingly challenging in today's complex and interconnected world. Geopolitical tensions arise from competing national interests, strategic rivalries, ideological differences, and historical grievances among countries. These tensions can hinder cooperation, impede decision-making processes, and undermine the effectiveness of multilateral institutions. However, effectively addressing and managing these tensions is crucial for promoting global stability, advancing shared interests, and finding collective solutions to global challenges. This paper explores the strategies and approaches that can be employed to effectively manage geopolitical tensions in multilateralism.

Understanding Geopolitical Tensions in Multilateralism

Geopolitical tensions in multilateralism emerge from a variety of sources, such as territorial disputes, ideological differences, economic competition, and power struggles among major powers. These tensions can manifest in various forms, including trade conflicts, military standoffs, diplomatic disputes, and ideological clashes. Geopolitical tensions often arise when countries perceive their interests to be threatened, their influence to be challenged, or when there are conflicting visions of global governance.

The Role of Multilateralism in Managing Geopolitical Tensions

Multilateralism provides a framework for countries to engage in dialogue, negotiation, and cooperation on global issues. Multilateral institutions, such as the United Nations (UN), World Trade

Organization (WTO), and regional organizations, serve as platforms for addressing geopolitical tensions and finding collective solutions. Through multilateralism, countries can engage in peaceful resolution of conflicts, build trust, and foster cooperation on areas of common interest.

Strategies for Managing Geopolitical Tensions

Dialogue and Diplomacy: Engaging in open and constructive dialogue is crucial for managing geopolitical tensions. Diplomatic channels, bilateral talks, and multilateral forums provide opportunities for countries to express concerns, understand perspectives, and find common ground. By promoting diplomatic engagement, countries can build trust, enhance communication, and identify areas of cooperation, even in the midst of tensions.

Conflict Resolution Mechanisms: Establishing effective conflict resolution mechanisms within multilateral institutions is essential for managing geopolitical tensions. Mediation, arbitration, and dispute settlement mechanisms can help de-escalate conflicts and find peaceful solutions. These mechanisms should be impartial, transparent, and trusted by all parties involved.

Inclusive Decision-Making: Ensuring inclusivity in decision-making processes can help address power imbalances and mitigate geopolitical tensions. Allowing diverse voices and perspectives to be heard promotes a sense of ownership and reduces feelings of marginalization. Inclusive decision-making also enhances the legitimacy and effectiveness of multilateral institutions.

Confidence-Building Measures: Confidence-building measures play a crucial role in managing geopolitical tensions. Building trust and confidence among countries can help reduce the likelihood of conflicts and encourage cooperation. Measures such as transparency, information sharing, joint projects, and cultural exchanges can contribute to building trust and fostering mutual understanding.

Economic Cooperation: Economic cooperation can be a powerful tool for managing geopolitical tensions. Trade, investment, and economic interdependence can create mutual benefits and incentives for countries to resolve conflicts peacefully. Economic cooperation initiatives, such as regional trade agreements and economic integration frameworks, can contribute to reducing tensions and promoting stability.

Normative Frameworks: Establishing and upholding normative frameworks within multilateral institutions can provide guidance for managing geopolitical tensions. Adhering to international law, human rights norms, and principles of good governance can help set standards of behavior and reduce conflicts. Norms also provide a common ground for countries to cooperate and find shared solutions.

Track II Diplomacy and Civil Society Engagement: Track II diplomacy, which involves non-governmental actors, academics, and civil society organizations, can play a significant role in managing geopolitical tensions. These actors can provide alternative perspectives, facilitate dialogue, and generate creative solutions outside traditional diplomatic channels. Engaging with civil society organizations and academic institutions can contribute to building bridges, promoting understanding, and fostering cooperation among nations.

Strategic Partnerships: **Building strategic partnerships with like-minded countries can help manage geopolitical tensions. Forming alliances or coalitions based on shared values and interests can provide support and solidarity in addressing common challenges. Strategic partnerships can amplify the voices of countries with shared concerns and promote collective action.

Confidence-Building Measures: Confidence-building measures play a crucial role in managing geopolitical tensions. Building trust and confidence among countries can help reduce the likelihood of conflicts and encourage cooperation. Measures such as transparency, information sharing, joint projects, and cultural exchanges can contribute to building trust and fostering mutual understanding.

Leadership and Mediation: Effective leadership and mediation skills are vital in managing geopolitical tensions. Skilled mediators can facilitate dialogue, bridge gaps, and find common ground. Leaders who prioritize diplomacy, negotiation, and compromise can set a positive tone and demonstrate a commitment to peaceful resolution of conflicts.

Challenges and Limitations

While the strategies mentioned above can help manage geopolitical tensions in multilateralism, there are challenges and limitations that need to be acknowledged:

Power Dynamics: Power imbalances among countries can hinder effective management of geopolitical tensions. Dominant powers may exert undue influence, and smaller nations may feel marginalized or unheard. Addressing power dynamics and ensuring equal participation and representation is crucial for effective multilateralism.

Divergent Interests: Countries have diverse interests, which can sometimes be difficult to reconcile. Conflicting interests may hinder cooperation and compromise, leading to persistent tensions. Balancing competing interests requires skillful negotiation and a willingness to find win-win solutions.

Lack of Trust: Deep-rooted mistrust among nations can impede efforts to manage geopolitical tensions. Historical grievances, territorial disputes, and ideological differences can create a climate of suspicion. Rebuilding trust requires time, consistent actions, and a commitment to open dialogue.

Non-Compliance: The effectiveness of multilateral institutions depends on the willingness of countries to comply with their decisions and commitments. Non-compliance or selective compliance can undermine the legitimacy and credibility of multilateralism. Strengthening compliance mechanisms is essential for managing tensions effectively.

Nationalist and Populist Movements: The rise of nationalist and populist movements in some countries can complicate efforts to manage geopolitical tensions. These movements often prioritize national interests over multilateral cooperation, leading to increased polarization and confrontations. Navigating these dynamics requires strategic diplomacy and a focus on the long-term benefits of multilateralism.

Managing geopolitical tensions in multilateralism is a complex and ongoing challenge. However, it is essential for promoting global stability, fostering cooperation, and addressing shared challenges. By employing strategies such as dialogue and diplomacy, inclusive decision-making, economic cooperation, and confidence-building measures, countries can work towards managing tensions effectively. It requires leadership, trust-building, and a commitment to the principles of multilateralism. By actively engaging in conflict resolution, upholding normative frameworks, and building strategic partnerships, countries can contribute to a more peaceful and cooperative international order. Multilateralism remains a vital tool in addressing geopolitical tensions and creating a world characterized by mutual understanding, cooperation, and shared prosperity.

Chinese Perception and Trust Building

Perception and trust are two crucial elements that shape the dynamics of international relations. How a nation is perceived by others and the level of trust it can build with other countries play a significant role in determining its influence, credibility, and ability to achieve its foreign policy objectives. In the case of China, a rising global power, understanding its perception and efforts to build trust is essential for comprehending its interactions with the international community. This paper explores the Chinese perception of its role in the world and examines the strategies and challenges it faces in building trust with other nations.

Chinese Perception of its Role:

China's perception of its role in the world has evolved significantly over time. Historically, China has viewed itself as a "Middle Kingdom," a central civilization surrounded by lesser states. This perception fostered a sense of cultural and political superiority, leading to a relatively insular approach to international relations. However, in recent decades, China has undergone a transformation from a closed economy to an emerging global power with aspirations of becoming a global leader.

China's perception of its role in the world is shaped by several factors. Firstly, its historical and cultural legacy plays a significant role in its self-perception. China's long history, rich cultural heritage, and the notion of being the "Central Kingdom" contribute to a sense of pride and confidence in its position on the global stage.

Secondly, China's economic rise and growing global influence have fueled a perception of itself as a major global power. Its rapid economic growth, massive market potential, and increasing investments in other countries through initiatives like the Belt and Road Initiative (BRI) have bolstered China's perception of itself as a key player in shaping the global order.

Additionally, China's perception is shaped by its desire to be recognized as a responsible global actor. China emphasizes its commitment to peaceful development, non-interference in the internal affairs of other countries, and the pursuit of win-win cooperation. It presents itself as a champion of multilateralism, advocating for a more equitable and inclusive international system.

Strategies for Building Trust:

Building trust with other nations is crucial for China's foreign policy objectives and its long-term aspirations as a global power. To enhance its credibility and foster trust, China employs several strategies:

Economic Diplomacy: China's economic diplomacy is a central pillar of its trust-building efforts. It leverages its economic prowess to forge economic partnerships, invest in infrastructure projects, and provide development assistance to other countries. The BRI is a prime example of China's economic diplomacy, aiming to enhance connectivity, trade, and economic cooperation across regions. By engaging in mutually beneficial economic activities, China seeks to build trust and strengthen its relationships with partner nations.

Dialogue and Engagement: China places a strong emphasis on dialogue and engagement with other countries. It actively participates in multilateral institutions, such as the United Nations and regional organizations, to contribute to global governance and address global challenges. China's engagement with other nations through diplomatic exchanges, high-level visits, and people-to-people exchanges helps to build mutual understanding, address concerns, and foster trust.

Peaceful Development: China's commitment to peaceful development and non-interference is a key strategy for building trust. It emphasizes its adherence to the principles of sovereignty, territorial integrity, and non-interference in the internal affairs of other countries. China presents itself as a reliable partner, seeking cooperation and common ground rather than confrontation or aggression.

Cultural Diplomacy: China recognizes the power of cultural diplomacy in shaping perceptions and building trust. It promotes its rich cultural heritage, language, traditional practices, and soft power assets such as Confucius Institutes to enhance its global image and foster cultural exchanges. By promoting cultural understanding and appreciation, China aims to build bridges and strengthen people-to-people exchanges, which can contribute to trust-building between nations.

International Cooperation: China actively participates in international cooperation on various global issues, such as climate change, poverty alleviation, and public health. It contributes to global initiatives, such as the Paris Agreement on climate change and the Sustainable Development Goals, demonstrating its commitment to global challenges. Through collaborative efforts and shared responsibilities, China aims to build trust and demonstrate its willingness to work with other nations to address common concerns.

Challenges in Building Trust:

While China employs various strategies to build trust, it also faces significant challenges that can hinder its efforts:

Historical Perceptions and Misperceptions: China's historical legacy, particularly its perception as the "Middle Kingdom," can create misunderstandings and misperceptions among other nations. Some countries may view China's rise with suspicion, perceiving it as a potential threat to their own interests. Historical conflicts and territorial disputes further complicate trust-building efforts, as they can shape perceptions and breed mistrust.

Lack of Transparency: China's lack of transparency in certain areas, such as its military capabilities, foreign policies, and economic practices, can contribute to mistrust. The lack of transparency raises concerns among other nations regarding China's intentions and future trajectory. Greater transparency in areas such as military expenditures and strategic intentions could help address these concerns and build trust.

Human Rights Concerns: China's approach to human rights, freedom of expression, and governance has been a subject of criticism and concern in the international community. The perceived restrictions on civil liberties, internet censorship, and treatment of ethnic and religious minorities raise questions about China's commitment to universal values and human rights standards. These concerns can undermine trust-building efforts, especially with countries that prioritize human rights and democratic norms.

Geopolitical Rivalries: China's rising power and its growing influence have led to geopolitical rivalries with other major powers, most notably the United States. Competing strategic interests, trade disputes, and ideological differences can strain trust-building efforts. Geopolitical tensions can create a zero-sum perception among countries, making it challenging to build trust and cooperation.

Assertive Behavior: China's assertive behavior in certain territorial disputes, such as in the South

China Sea, has raised concerns among neighboring countries and the international community. Perceived aggressive actions, such as militarization of disputed islands and unilateral claims, can erode trust and escalate tensions. China's ability to address these concerns through peaceful dialogue and cooperative approaches is essential for trust-building.

Chinese perception and trust-building are vital aspects of its engagement with the international community. China's self-perception as a rising global power, its economic diplomacy, commitment to peaceful development, and engagement in multilateral institutions demonstrate its efforts to build trust and shape a positive image. However, challenges such as historical perceptions, lack of transparency, human rights concerns, geopolitical rivalries, and assertive behavior can impede trust-building efforts.

To overcome these challenges, China needs to demonstrate greater transparency, engage in meaningful dialogue, address human rights concerns, and promote peaceful resolution of disputes. Building trust requires consistency, openness, and a willingness to understand and accommodate the concerns and interests of other nations. By actively addressing these challenges and fostering mutual understanding, China can enhance trust, strengthen its relationships, and contribute positively to the stability and cooperation in the global community.

Chinese Soft Power and Public Diplomacy: Expanding Influence in a Globalized World

Chinese soft power and public diplomacy have emerged as critical components of China's strategy to expand its influence in the international arena. As China rises as a global power, it recognizes the importance of shaping its image and promoting its values, culture, and policies to the world. This paper provides a comprehensive analysis of Chinese soft power and public diplomacy efforts, exploring their objectives, tools, challenges, and impact. By examining various case studies and scholarly perspectives, this study seeks to shed light on the multifaceted nature of China's soft power and its implications for the global balance of power.

In an increasingly interconnected and globalized world, the concept of soft power has gained prominence in international relations. Coined by Joseph Nye, soft power refers to a country's ability to influence others through attraction, rather than coercion or force. It encompasses a nation's cultural, ideological, and institutional appeal, enabling it to shape international outcomes in its favor. As China rises as a global power, it recognizes the significance of soft power in enhancing its international influence and managing its image on the world stage. This paper delves into the multifaceted dimensions of Chinese soft power and explores its implications for China's aspirations in global politics.

The Evolution of Chinese Soft Power

China's approach to soft power has evolved over time, reflecting both internal developments and shifts in global politics. Historically, China's focus was primarily on consolidating its domestic strength and maintaining stability. However, with its rapid economic growth and increasing global engagement, China has acknowledged the importance of shaping its image abroad.

China's perception of soft power has also undergone transformations. Initially, Chinese leaders viewed soft power as a Western concept imposed upon China, associated with cultural imperialism and an attempt to undermine its political system. However, over time, Chinese policymakers have come to recognize the value of soft power in advancing national interests and have adopted a more proactive approach to its development.

Several factors have influenced China's soft power strategy. Firstly, the desire to project a positive image and counter negative perceptions of China's rise plays a crucial role. China aims to present itself as a responsible global player, committed to peace, development, and cooperation. Secondly, China seeks to enhance its cultural influence and promote its rich history, traditions, and values to the world. By doing so, it aims to foster a sense of affinity and understanding with other nations. Thirdly, China's soft power efforts are closely linked to its economic and political objectives. It leverages its economic might and development assistance programs to enhance its influence and gain support on global issues.

Objectives of Chinese Soft Power

The objectives of Chinese soft power are multi-fold and interconnected. Firstly, China seeks to shape a positive international image and improve its global reputation. It aims to be seen as a responsible global power that contributes to international development, peace, and stability. By projecting an image of goodwill and cooperation, China hopes to build trust and gain acceptance among the international community.

Secondly, cultural influence and soft power projection are significant objectives for China. China possesses a rich cultural heritage, including its traditions, arts, cuisine, and philosophy. It seeks to promote Chinese culture globally through cultural diplomacy, educational exchange programs, and the establishment of cultural institutions like Confucius Institutes. By sharing its cultural values and traditions, China aims to enhance its soft power and foster cultural understanding between nations.

Thirdly, countering negative narratives and perceptions about China is an essential objective. China has faced criticism and skepticism regarding its political system, human rights record, and assertive foreign policy. It endeavors to counter such narratives and present an alternative narrative that emphasizes its achievements, peaceful development, and contributions to global governance.

Lastly, Chinese soft power efforts are closely intertwined with its economic and political objectives. China leverages its economic resources, foreign aid, and investment programs to build relationships and influence outcomes. By positioning itself as a key contributor to global economic development, China aims to gain support for its political positions and expand its geopolitical influence.

Tools and Instruments of Chinese Soft Power

Confucius Institutes and language promotion: Confucius Institutes are educational institutions established by the Chinese government to promote Chinese language and culture. They operate in numerous countries and serve as platforms for cultural exchange and language learning. By disseminating Chinese language and culture, China aims to enhance its cultural influence and attract students and scholars to study in China.

Media and information dissemination: China recognizes the importance of controlling its narrative and has invested heavily in expanding its global media presence. State-owned media outlets like Xinhua, China Central Television (CCTV), and China Global Television Network (CGTN) disseminate news, information, and entertainment content worldwide. Through these channels, China seeks to shape international perceptions, counter negative narratives, and present its perspective on global issues.

Cultural diplomacy and exchange programs: **China** actively promotes cultural diplomacy through various means, including cultural exchange programs, art exhibitions, music and dance performances, and film festivals. By showcasing its cultural heritage and contemporary achievements in arts and entertainment, China aims to foster cultural understanding, appreciation, and admiration.

Development assistance and economic cooperation: China's economic engagement with other nations plays a crucial role in its soft power strategy. The Belt and Road Initiative (BRI), a massive infrastructure and connectivity project, serves as a platform for economic cooperation and development assistance. By providing financial aid,investment, and infrastructure development to partner countries, China seeks to build long-term relationships, enhance its influence, and improve its global image as a responsible economic powerhouse.

Public diplomacy campaigns and branding efforts: China actively engages in public diplomacy campaigns to promote its values, policies, and achievements. This includes hosting international conferences and forums, organizing cultural events and exhibitions, and launching media campaigns. China also employs branding strategies to enhance its national image, such as the "Made in China 2025" initiative, which aims to reposition China as a global leader in high-tech industries.
Challenges and Criticisms

While China's soft power efforts have made significant strides, they face several challenges and criticisms that can impede their effectiveness. These include:

Perceptions of China's political system and human rights record: China's authoritarian political system and its human rights record have been a subject of contention and criticism in the international community. These factors can undermine the appeal of China's soft power initiatives, particularly among countries that prioritize democratic values and human rights.

Assertive foreign policy and territorial disputes: China's assertive foreign policy, particularly in territorial disputes in the South China Sea and with Taiwan, has raised concerns among neighboring countries and affected its regional soft power. Its aggressive actions can erode trust, create tensions, and hinder its ability to build positive relationships in the region.

Communication and language barriers: China faces challenges in effectively communicating its messages to global audiences due to language barriers and differences in cultural context. Language limitations can limit the reach and impact of China's soft power initiatives, particularly in regions where English is the dominant language.

Cultural differences and misunderstandings: China's cultural values, norms, and practices may differ significantly from those of other countries. This can lead to misunderstandings, misperceptions, and cultural clashes, which can affect the reception of China's soft power efforts.

The impact of the COVID-19 pandemic: The COVID-19 pandemic has had both positive and negative implications for China's soft power. China's provision of medical assistance, supplies, and vaccines to other countries has been viewed as a positive contribution. However, criticisms of China's initial handling of the outbreak and allegations of misinformation have also damaged its global reputation.

Case Studies: Chinese Soft Power in Action

Examining specific case studies provides insight into how China's soft power strategies are implemented and their impact. Some notable examples include:

Belt and Road Initiative (BRI) and infrastructure projects: The BRI is China's flagship soft power initiative, aiming to enhance connectivity and economic cooperation across Asia, Europe, Africa, and beyond. Through investments in infrastructure projects, China seeks to deepen its economic ties, gain influence, and shape regional development.

Cultural diplomacy: Chinese cinema and entertainment industry: Chinese cinema has gained international recognition in recent years, with films like "Crouching Tiger, Hidden Dragon" and "Wolf Warrior 2" achieving global success. By promoting its film industry, China projects its culture, values, and artistic achievements, contributing to its soft power appeal.

: Confucius Institutes have been established in many countries as a platform for Chinese language education and cultural exchange. These institutes serve as vehicles for promoting Chinese culture and attracting students to study in China, contributing to China's cultural influence and soft power projection.

: China's provision of COVID-19 vaccines and medical assistance to countries in need has been a significant soft power strategy during the pandemic. By positioning itself as a global health provider, China aims to strengthen its ties, gain goodwill, and improve its global image.

The Impact of Chinese Soft Power

Assessing the impact of Chinese soft power is complex, as it operates on multiple fronts and involves a range of stakeholders and variables.

Nevertheless, it is possible to identify some key elements of the impact of Chinese soft power efforts:

Regional and global responses to Chinese influence: China's soft power initiatives have elicited a range of responses from different regions and countries. Some countries have welcomed Chinese investment, economic cooperation, and cultural exchanges, viewing them as opportunities for development and mutually beneficial partnerships. Others, however, have expressed concerns about the potential implications of China's rising influence, particularly regarding its political and economic motivations.

Competition and cooperation with Western soft power: China's soft power ambitions have put it in competition with established Western powers, such as the United States and European countries, who have traditionally dominated the global soft power landscape. China's rising influence has led to a reevaluation of the balance of power in international relations, as it seeks to establish alternative narratives and norms to challenge Western dominance.

Perception and image improvement: Chinese soft power efforts have contributed to improving China's global image to some extent. Through cultural exchanges, media engagement, and economic cooperation, China has been able to project a more positive and multifaceted image. However, challenges such as political controversies and human rights concerns continue to impact perceptions of China, particularly in the West.

Influence on public opinion and discourse: Chinese soft power initiatives have influenced public opinion and discourse on various global issues. By shaping narratives and providing alternative perspectives, China has sought to gain support for its policies and positions. However, debates and discussions around China's rise and its intentions have also become more nuanced and critical in many parts of the world.

Future Prospects and Implications

Looking ahead, Chinese soft power faces both challenges and opportunities. Some key factors and implications for the future include:

Challenges: China's soft power efforts will continue to face challenges related to perceptions of its political system, human rights record, and assertive foreign policy. China will need to address these concerns effectively to build trust and enhance its soft power appeal. Language and cultural barriers also present ongoing challenges, particularly in reaching global audiences. Furthermore, competition from Western soft power, changing geopolitical dynamics, and evolving global issues such as climate change and technology governance will shape China's soft power landscape.

: China's economic and technological advancements provide significant opportunities for enhancing its soft power. By leveraging its economic resources, innovation, and development assistance, China can position itself as a key contributor to global issues, such as sustainable development and climate change mitigation. Additionally, the increasing role of digital diplomacy and technology offers new avenues for China to engage with global audiences and shape international narratives.

Balancing soft power and hard power: China will need to navigate the delicate balance between soft power and hard power in its foreign policy. While soft power can enhance China's influence and shape its global image, it must be complemented by responsible behavior, respect for international norms, and effective diplomacy. The strategic alignment of soft power and hard power will be crucial for China's long-term objectives and its relationships with other major powers.

Chinese soft power and public diplomacy have emerged as integral elements of China's strategy to expand its influence and shape its global image. By leveraging its cultural heritage, economic strength, and development assistance, China aims to project a positive international image, promote its values, and enhance its geopolitical influence. However, China faces challenges such as political controversies, human rights concerns, and communication barriers that impact the effectiveness of its soft power initiatives. The future prospects of Chinese soft power will be shaped by how China addresses these challenges, navigates global dynamics, and balances soft power with hard power in its foreign policy approach. Understanding Chinese soft power is crucial for comprehending the evolving global balance of power and the implications for international relations in the 21st century.

Challenges in Perception Management

Perception management is a critical component of modern statecraft, aimed at shaping and influencing public opinion domestically and internationally. It involves the use of various strategies and tactics to shape narratives, control information flows, and project a desired image to achieve specific goals. China, as a rising global power, faces significant challenges in perception management due to various factors such as its political system, global influence, and international reputation. This article explores the challenges that China encounters in perception management and analyzes the implications for its domestic and foreign policies.

The Chinese Political System and Media Control:

One of the primary challenges China faces in perception management is its political system, characterized by strict state control and censorship. The Chinese Communist Party (CCP) exercises tight control over media and communication channels, limiting the free flow of information and shaping narratives to align with the party's interests. The Great Firewall, a sophisticated system of internet censorship, blocks access to foreign websites and social media platforms, preventing Chinese citizens from accessing alternative viewpoints.

This media control creates a challenge for China in managing its domestic perception. Despite efforts to promote positive narratives about economic development and national unity, the CCP's authoritarian image and human rights concerns are difficult to conceal. Social media and online platforms, although monitored and censored, provide avenues for dissent and alternative narratives, making it challenging for the Chinese government to control the narrative entirely.

Information Warfare and Disinformation:

China also faces challenges in managing its perception on the global stage, particularly concerning information warfare and disinformation campaigns. As China seeks to expand its influence and shape international narratives, it has been accused of engaging in disinformation campaigns, spreading propaganda, and using social media manipulation to promote its interests. These activities aim to undermine trust in Western institutions, deflect criticism of Chinese policies, and project a positive image of China's rise.

However, China's efforts in information warfare face several challenges. First, the global community, particularly the United States and its allies, have become increasingly aware of Chinese disinformation tactics and are actively countering them. The exposure of Chinese influence campaigns, such as the manipulation of social media platforms, has led to increased scrutiny and a diminished impact of these efforts. Second, the diverse and decentralized nature of media landscapes worldwide makes it challenging for China to control narratives effectively in different regions and cultures.

Human Rights Concerns and International Backlash:

China's human rights record, particularly regarding issues such as the treatment of Uighur Muslims in Xinjiang and the crackdown on democratic movements in Hong Kong, poses significant challenges to its perception management efforts. The international community, human rights organizations, and independent media outlets have raised serious concerns about these issues, leading to a negative perception of China's government and policies.

Despite China's attempts to control the narrative through state-controlled media and propaganda, human rights violations have gained global attention. The dissemination of evidence, eyewitness accounts, and reports from international organizations has resulted in increased international backlash and condemnation. This has created a significant challenge for China in managing its international image and countering negative perceptions associated with its human rights practices.

Nationalism and Public Opinion:

Nationalism presents both opportunities and challenges for China's perception management. The Chinese government often utilizes nationalist sentiments to bolster support for its policies and project an image of national strength and unity. However, nationalism can also become a double-edged sword, leading to public opinion that is difficult to control or predict.

When nationalist sentiments are directed against foreign entities or nations, it can lead to an aggressive or confrontational stance, which may negatively impact China's international relations and reputation. Instances of online nationalist movements, "wolf warrior diplomacy," and boycotts targeting foreign companies have at times created challenges for China's perception management efforts, as they are seen as overly nationalistic and antagonistic.

Chinese Building Trust and Enhancing Cooperation: A Strategic Approach to Global Partnerships

China's emergence as a global powerhouse has transformed its role in the international arena. As the world's second-largest economy and a significant player in global affairs, China recognizes the importance of building trust and enhancing cooperation with other nations. In recent years, the Chinese government has adopted a strategic approach to foster positive relationships and establish mutually beneficial partnerships. This essay will explore China's efforts in building trust and enhancing cooperation on various fronts, including economic, diplomatic, and cultural dimensions.

I. **Economic Cooperation**:

China's economic prowess is well-known, and it has actively sought to leverage this strength to enhance global cooperation. The Belt and Road Initiative (BRI), launched in 2013, is a prime example of China's commitment to promoting economic connectivity and cooperation. The BRI aims to improve infrastructure, trade, and investment links between China and countries along the ancient Silk Road routes. By facilitating the construction of ports, railways, and other infrastructure projects, China seeks to foster economic growth and development, while also building trust and fostering closer ties with partner countries.

Additionally, China has taken steps to enhance regional economic integration. The establishment of the Asian Infrastructure Investment Bank (AIIB) in 2015 exemplifies this approach. The AIIB, with its focus on financing infrastructure projects in Asia, provides an alternative platform for countries to collaborate on development initiatives. China's active participation and financial contributions to the AIIB demonstrate its commitment to regional economic cooperation and its willingness to work with other nations to address common challenges.

II. **Diplomatic Cooperation**:

China has recognized the importance of diplomacy in building trust and cooperation. The concept of "win-win cooperation" is central to China's diplomatic approach. By emphasizing mutual benefit and equality in its engagements, China seeks to build trust and cultivate long-term partnerships.

China's diplomatic efforts extend beyond traditional alliances. It has actively engaged in multilateral forums, such as the United Nations, where it has sought to promote cooperation and address global challenges. China's participation in peacekeeping operations, its contributions to UN development programs, and its support for international agreements like the Paris Climate Accord highlight its commitment to global cooperation and collective action.

Furthermore, China has pursued a policy of "neighborhood diplomacy" to enhance relations with neighboring countries. Through initiatives like the Forum on China-Africa Cooperation (FOCAC) and the China-ASEAN (Association of Southeast Asian Nations) cooperation framework, China has deepened economic ties and strengthened diplomatic relations. By engaging in dialogue and collaboration, China aims to foster trust and goodwill among its neighbors, promoting regional stability and economic integration.

III. **Cultural Exchanges**:

Cultural exchanges play a crucial role in building understanding, fostering trust, and enhancing cooperation between nations. China recognizes this and has made significant efforts to promote cultural exchanges on a global scale. The Confucius Institutes, established around the world, serve as hubs for promoting Chinese language, culture, and education. These institutes facilitate academic and cultural exchanges, enabling people from different countries to learn about China, its traditions, and its people. By nurturing cultural understanding and appreciation, China aims to build bridges and strengthen relationships with other nations.

Furthermore, China has been proactive in hosting international events and cultural festivals, such as the Beijing Olympics in 2008 and the Belt and Road Forum for International Cooperation. These events provide platforms for cultural exchange, allowing countries to showcase their traditions, foster people-to-people connections, and promote mutual understanding. Such cultural engagements contribute to building trust and creating a shared sense of community among nations.

IV. Science and Technological Collaboration:

China's rise as a global technological powerhouse has created opportunities for enhanced cooperation in the field of science and technology. The Chinese government has recognized the importance of innovation and collaboration in driving economic growth and technological advancement. China has actively sought to strengthen partnerships and promote cooperation in science and technology through various initiatives.

One notable initiative is the establishment of research and innovation centers, such as the China-EU Research and Innovation Center, China-US Innovation Center, and China-UK Innovation and Entrepreneurship Competition. These centers provide platforms for researchers, entrepreneurs, and innovators from different countries to collaborate, share knowledge, and develop joint projects. By fostering international collaboration, China aims to leverage global expertise and resources to drive innovation and technological progress.

Moreover, China has been actively engaging in international scientific collaborations and initiatives. For instance, the Chinese government has invested significantly in space exploration, partnering with other countries on space missions and research projects. China's participation in the International Space Station (ISS) program and its successful lunar exploration missions, including the Chang'e program, demonstrate its commitment to scientific cooperation and knowledge sharing in space exploration.

China has also made significant strides in emerging technologies such as artificial intelligence (AI), 5G telecommunications, and renewable energy.

Through research partnerships, technology transfer, and joint ventures, China has sought to collaborate with other countries in these fields. By sharing expertise and resources, China aims to advance technological frontiers while building trust and fostering cooperation.

V. **Environmental Cooperation**:

Recognizing the importance of global environmental challenges, China has placed increasing emphasis on environmental cooperation and sustainable development. The Chinese government has made significant commitments to combat climate change and promote environmental conservation.

China's leadership in renewable energy development is noteworthy. As the world's largest producer of solar panels and wind turbines, China has taken significant steps to transition towards cleaner and more sustainable energy sources. The country has also demonstrated its commitment to international cooperation in this domain. For instance, China has collaborated with other countries on joint research projects, knowledge exchange, and capacity building in renewable energy.

Furthermore, China has actively participated in global climate change negotiations and initiatives. It has ratified the Paris Agreement and set ambitious targets for reducing greenhouse gas emissions. China's engagement in multilateral forums such as the United Nations Framework Convention on Climate Change (UNFCCC) showcases its commitment to global environmental cooperation. By actively contributing to global efforts to address climate change, China aims to build trust and strengthen cooperation with other nations in tackling this shared challenge.

VI. **Challenges and Opportunities**:

While China's efforts to build trust and enhance cooperation are commendable, they are not without challenges. One significant challenge is the perception of China's growing influence and its impact on global power dynamics. Some countries express concerns about China's intentions and question its adherence to international norms and rules. China must address these concerns by engaging in transparent and responsible behavior, promoting dialogue, and actively addressing global issues in a cooperative manner.

Another challenge lies in navigating geopolitical tensions and competing interests among nations. In an increasingly interconnected and interdependent world, cooperation requires compromise and understanding. China must navigate complex geopolitical dynamics, respect the sovereignty of other nations, and find common ground to foster cooperation.

However, these challenges also present opportunities for China to demonstrate its commitment to building trust and enhancing cooperation. By actively engaging in dialogue, promoting inclusivity, and addressing concerns with openness and transparency, China can foster understanding and build stronger partnerships.

China's rise as a global power necessitates a strategic approach to building trust and enhancing cooperation with other nations. Through economic cooperation, diplomatic engagement, cultural exchanges, scientific collaborations, and environmental initiatives, China has taken significant steps to foster positive relationships and establish mutually beneficial partnerships. By embracing the principles of mutual benefit, equality, and win-win cooperation, China has the potential to shape a more cooperative and interconnected world. However, challenges persist, and it is essential for China to navigate them with sensitivity and openness. As China continues to play a significant role in global affairs, its commitment to building trust and enhancing cooperation will be crucial in shaping a peaceful and prosperous world order. By building trust and fostering cooperation, China can contribute to the stability and prosperity of the global community while promoting its own interests.

As the world's second-largest economy and a rising global power, China's actions have significant implications for global affairs. By actively engaging with other nations and promoting cooperation, China can leverage its economic and political influence to shape a more stable, prosperous, and interconnected world. Moreover, by embracing a cooperative approach to international relations, China can build trust and understanding among nations, which is essential for addressing global challenges and promoting sustainable development.

In conclusion, building trust and enhancing cooperation are critical for China's continued rise as a global power. By pursuing a strategic approach that emphasizes mutual benefit, equality, and win-win cooperation, China can foster positive relationships with other nations and contribute to the stability and prosperity of the global community. As China's role in global affairs continues to evolve, its commitment to building trust and enhancing cooperation will be increasingly vital in shaping a more cooperative, inclusive, and interconnected world.

Assessing China's Multilateralism

China's approach to multilateralism has become increasingly significant in recent years as the country has gained economic and political influence on the global stage. China's participation in multilateral institutions and its promotion of initiatives like the Belt and Road Initiative (BRI) have garnered both praise and criticism. In this section, we will assess China's multilateralism by examining its achievements, criticisms, and future prospects and challenges.

China's multilateralism has undergone significant scrutiny, with both achievements and criticisms shaping its trajectory. The Belt and Road Initiative (BRI) stands as a prominent achievement, fostering connectivity and economic cooperation among participating countries through infrastructure projects. Additionally, China's active participation in multilateral institutions like the United Nations (UN) and its contributions to regional development banks such as the Asian Infrastructure Investment Bank (AIIB) have allowed China to influence global governance.

However, criticisms have also been leveled against China's multilateralism. Concerns exist regarding China's adherence to international norms, particularly with regards to human rights and governance practices. Some argue that China's domestic policies, such as limitations on freedom of expression and minority rights, clash with the principles upheld by multilateral institutions.

The expansion of China's influence has generated apprehension about its intentions and potential for geopolitical dominance. Critics contend that China's multilateral initiatives, including the BRI, primarily serve its own strategic interests rather than genuine global cooperation. The financial implications and transparency of BRI projects have raised skepticism, as some participating countries face debt burdens and questions about the sustainability of the projects.

China's assertive behavior in territorial disputes, notably in the South China Sea, has also drawn criticism. Such actions challenge the principles of multilateralism, including the United Nations Convention on the Law of the Sea (UNCLOS) and the peaceful resolution of disputes.

Looking ahead, China's multilateralism faces both prospects and challenges. China's growing economic and political influence positions it as a key player in shaping global governance and addressing shared challenges. Collaboration with other countries and institutions, including in areas such as trade reform and technological innovation, presents prospects for constructive multilateral engagement.

Nonetheless, challenges persist. Ongoing tensions between China and some Western democracies, driven by geopolitical competition and differing values, may hinder effective multilateral cooperation. Balancing China's rise with the interests of other countries is essential for fostering productive relationships.

Moreover, China must address concerns regarding its domestic policies and practices, particularly related to human.

10.1 Achievements and Criticisms

10.1.1 Achievements

China has made notable achievements in the realm of multilateralism. One of its significant accomplishments is its active participation in various multilateral institutions, including the United Nations (UN), World Trade Organization (WTO), and Asian Infrastructure Investment Bank (AIIB). China's involvement in these institutions has allowed it to shape global governance rules and contribute to decision-making processes.

Additionally, China's BRI has been lauded as a major multilateral initiative aimed at enhancing connectivity and promoting economic cooperation among participating countries. The BRI has led to infrastructure development projects, trade facilitation, and people-to-people exchanges in numerous regions. China's financial contributions to multilateral development banks, such as the AIIB, have also increased its influence in global economic affairs.

Furthermore, China has taken on leadership roles in addressing global challenges, such as climate change. The country has committed to the Paris Agreement and has become the world's largest investor in renewable energy. Its engagement in climate negotiations and initiatives like the Belt and Road Initiative International Green Development Coalition have demonstrated its commitment to multilateral efforts in combating climate change.

10.1.2 Criticisms

Despite its achievements, China's multilateralism has faced several criticisms. One key criticism revolves around concerns over China's adherence to international norms and principles, particularly regarding human rights and governance. Critics argue that China's domestic policies, such as restrictions on freedom of expression and repression of minority groups, undermine its commitment to the values upheld by many multilateral institutions.

Furthermore, China's expanding influence has raised concerns about its intent and potential for geopolitical dominance. Some argue that China's multilateral initiatives, such as the BRI, are driven by its own strategic interests rather than a genuine desire for global cooperation. The debt burdens faced by some participating countries and concerns about the sustainability and transparency of BRI projects have further fueled skepticism.

China's assertive behavior in territorial disputes, such as in the South China Sea, has also drawn criticism. Its actions have been seen as challenging the principles of multilateralism, particularly with regards to the United Nations Convention on the Law of the Sea (UNCLOS) and the peaceful resolution of disputes.

10.2 Future Prospects and Challenges

China's multilateralism will face both prospects and challenges in the future. The following are key considerations:

10.2.1 **Prospects**

China's growing economic and political influence positions it as a significant player in shaping global governance and multilateral initiatives. Its continued engagement in multilateral institutions provides opportunities for cooperation on global challenges such as climate change, poverty reduction, and public health.

Moreover, China has shown willingness to work with other countries and institutions in developing common rules and norms. For example, it has expressed support for reforming the World Trade Organization and has contributed to the development of regional trade agreements like the Regional Comprehensive Economic Partnership

(RCEP). These efforts signal China's potential for constructive multilateral engagement.

Additionally, China's advancements in technology and innovation can contribute to global cooperation, particularly in areas such as renewable energy, artificial intelligence, and digital governance. By sharing its expertise and collaborating with other countries, China can contribute to the development of global norms and standards.

10.2.2 Challenges

China's multilateralism also faces significant challenges. One major challenge
is the ongoing tensions between China and some Western democracies. The geopolitical competition, trade disputes, and differing views on human rights and governance have strained China's relationships with countries such as the United States and several European nations. These tensions can hinder

China's ability to effectively promote its multilateral initiatives and garner broad support.

Furthermore, China's rise as a global power has created concerns among some countries about a potential power imbalance. The fear of China's dominance and its impact on the existing international order has led to calls for greater scrutiny of China's actions and intentions. Balancing China's growing influence with the interests of other countries will be a critical challenge for effective multilateral cooperation.

Moreover, China's domestic policies and practices, particularly in relation to human rights, could continue to pose challenges to its multilateral engagement. The divergence between China's approach and the values upheld by many multilateral institutions may create tensions and hinder collaboration on key issues.

Another challenge lies in ensuring the transparency and sustainability of China's multilateral initiatives, particularly the BRI. Addressing concerns about debt sustainability, environmental impact, and governance standards will be crucial in gaining broader trust and support for China's initiatives.

Additionally, navigating complex regional dynamics will be essential for China's multilateralism. China's interactions with neighboring countries, especially in territorial disputes, can significantly impact its credibility as a multilateral partner. Resolving these disputes peacefully and in accordance with international law will be crucial for fostering regional stability and cooperation.

In conclusion, China's multilateralism has seen both achievements and criticisms. China's active participation in multilateral institutions, its promotion of the BRI, and its leadership on global issues like climate change have been notable achievements. However, concerns about China's adherence to international norms, its expanding influence, and its assertive behavior have raised criticisms and skepticism. The future prospects of China's multilateralism will depend on its ability to address these challenges, engage in constructive dialogue with other countries, and demonstrate a genuine commitment to shared values and principles. Effective multilateral cooperation with China has the potential to contribute to global governance, economic development, and the resolution of common challenges.

Glossary:

Belt and Road Initiative (BRI): A large-scale infrastructure development and investment project launched by China in 2013. It aims to enhance connectivity and promote economic cooperation among participating countries through the construction of roads, railways, ports, and other infrastructure projects.

Asian Infrastructure Investment Bank (AIIB): A multilateral development bank established in 2016 with the goal of financing infrastructure projects in the Asia-Pacific region. China is a founding member of the AIIB and has played a significant role in its operations.

United Nations (UN): An international organization founded in 1945, composed of member states committed to promoting peace, security, and cooperation. The UN serves as a forum for member countries to discuss and address global issues, ranging from human rights to climate change.

World Trade Organization (WTO): An international organization that oversees global trade rules and resolves trade disputes among member countries. It provides a platform for negotiations and agreements on trade liberalization and the development of international trade regulations.

Paris Agreement: An international treaty adopted in 2015 under the United Nations Framework Convention on Climate Change (UNFCCC). The agreement aims to combat climate change by limiting global warming to well below 2 degrees Celsius above pre-industrial levels and pursuing efforts to limit the temperature increase to 1.5 degrees Celsius.

References:

Xinhua. (2019). China's AIIB becomes positive force in multilateralism. Xinhua. Retrieved from http://www.xinhuanet.com/english/2019-01/16/c _137745016.htm

The World Bank. (2021). Belt and Road Initiative. The World Bank. Retrieved from https://www.worldbank.org/en/topic/regional-in tegration/brief/belt-and-road-initiative

United Nations. (n.d.). About the UN. United Nations. Retrieved from https://www.un.org/en/about us

World Trade Organization. (n.d.). Understanding the WTO: What is the WTO? World Trade Organization. Retrieved from https://www.wto.org/english/thewto_e/whatis_e /whatis_e.htm

United Nations Framework Convention on Climate Change. (2015). Paris Agreement. United Nations Framework Convention on Climate Change. Retrieved from https://unfccc.int/process-and-meetings/the-paris-agreement/the-paris-agreement

Regional Comprehensive Economic Partnership (RCEP): A free trade agreement among 15 Asia-Pacific countries, including China, signed in 2020. RCEP aims to enhance regional economic integration by reducing tariffs and trade barriers, promoting investment, and establishing common rules and standards.

Geopolitical competition: Refers to the competition between countries for influence and power in global politics. Geopolitical competition can manifest in various forms, such as economic rivalries, military tensions, and diplomatic maneuvering.

Power imbalance: The uneven distribution of power and influence among countries. A power imbalance can occur when one country or group of countries has significantly more resources, capabilities, or leverage than others, potentially leading to asymmetrical relationships and challenges in multilateral cooperation.

Human rights: Basic rights and freedoms to which all individuals are entitled, regardless of their nationality, race, gender, or other characteristics. Human rights include civil and political rights, such as freedom of speech and the right to a fair trial, as well as economic, social, and cultural rights, such as the right to education and healthcare.

Transparency: Refers to the openness, accountability, and availability of information in decision-making processes and the conduct of affairs. Transparent practices allow for scrutiny, understanding, and trust-building among stakeholders.

Sustainability: The concept of meeting present needs without compromising the ability of future generations to meet their own needs. In the context of multilateral initiatives, sustainability encompasses environmental, social, and economic considerations, aiming for long-term viability and positive impacts.

Territorial disputes: Conflicts or disagreements between countries over the ownership or control of specific geographic areas. Territorial disputes can arise from conflicting historical claims, differing interpretations of boundaries, or strategic interests.